AARON TAIT AND KAITLIN TAIT

Entrepreneurs that change lives

(and how to be one)

Copyright © 2024 by Aaron Tait and Kaitlin Tait

All rights reserved. No part of this publication may be reproduced, stored or transmitted in any form or by any means, electronic, mechanical, photocopying, recording, scanning, or otherwise without written permission from the publisher. It is illegal to copy this book, post it to a website, or distribute it by any other means without permission.

Aaron Tait and Kaitlin Tait asserts the moral right to be identified as the author of this work.

Designations used by companies to distinguish their products are often claimed as trademarks. All brand names and product names used in this book and on its cover are trade names, service marks, trademarks and registered trademarks of their respective owners. The publishers and the book are not associated with any product or vendor mentioned in this book. None of the companies referenced within the book have endorsed the book.

First edition

This book was professionally typeset on Reedsy. Find out more at reedsy.com

*For those who
have the spark*

Contents

Foreword ii
Preface iii
1 Chapter 1 1
2 Chapter 2 18
3 Chapter 3 24
4 Chapter 4 29
5 Chapter 5 48
6 Chapter 6 82
7 Chapter 7 99
8 Chapter 8 139
9 Chapter 9 152
10 Chapter 10 160
11 Chapter 11 171
12 Chapter 12 189
13 Chapter 13 221
14 Conclusion (but really it's just the beginning) 228
Also by Aaron Tait and Kaitlin Tait 232

Foreword

Kaitlin and Aaron Tait are co-founders of the global impact organization ygap.org (previously known as Spark International) and were the creators of ygap's impact model. Since 2010 they have supported thousands of early-stage impact entrepreneurs across the world to launch and grow businesses that make a difference and helped to build impact and startup programs for organizations, including entities of the United Nations, Microsoft, and Mastercard. They were jointly named as Australia's 2015 Social Entrepreneurs of the Year by the Foundation for Young Australians and hold seven degrees between them. Aaron is the co-founder of the education company Education Changemakers, which was acquired by technology unicorn Go1, and he is the co-author of two books, *Edupreneur* and the best-selling *Dream Team*. They live in Byron Bay, Australia, with their two sons, Atlas and Finn.

Preface

The spark ...

This thing ... It makes you care a lot.

Care so much that you will give almost everything you have for what you believe in.

By everything, we mean all your time. Your money. Significant parts of your life.

It will keep you up at night, searching for better ways to solve the problems you are so frustrated by.

It will keep you going through the worst of days and bring tears of satisfaction on the best of them.

It will give you the courage to start from nothing and build something great.

We call it "the spark," and we felt it more than a decade ago.

It saw us sell everything we owned and dedicate ten years of our lives to build something we believed in. It almost took our lives several times.

We've seen "the spark" in others in every corner of the world. It, too, has led them to become obsessed with an idea and, in turn, to change the lives of people in their communities, their countries, and their world. In the coming pages, you will hear more about them.

That spark of inspiration is what this book is about. If you've started reading, maybe you already have it. If you don't, we trust you will soon.

Once it is there, we'll help to pour fuel on it.

Who Is This Book For?

We have closely examined thousands of early-stage impact businesses over the last decade.

By early stage, we mean that they are operating on less than US$5,000 of revenue each year, and are often yet to reach more than a hundred customers meaningfully. Financially, it's a risky stage for us to engage with a venture, and for years, we've been asked if we are investing too early. Yet we continue to believe this is a vitally important moment in the life of an entrepreneur because the sparks of potential that exist here are worth trying to turn into a mighty flame. If those sparks fizzle out, it potentially means children are not going to school, clinics are not improving health, and small businesses are closing their doors and letting people go from life-changing jobs.

So, these early businesses matter.

We say that investing this early is like playing pickup basketball in the projects of Chicago, looking for the next Michael Jordan.

Most of the business ideas that we hear about come from passionate people who believe they are on to something special and who have been willing to put in a great deal of effort to try to make it work. And while we would love to do our small part to support all of them, the reality is that we've only ever been able to work closely with around a hundred annually across Asia, Africa, and the Pacific through the programs that we run at ygap. Over the years, here is what we see playing out.

-More than half of them will not find a way to grow their business to a point that makes sense to continue, so they will close their doors, or keep it going only as a part-time side hustle. Their spark will stay small or be extinguished by a raindrop of a changing market, or the need to find a more stable paycheck rather than take the risk that comes with entrepreneurship. To be honest, at some point, this will be most of us who choose to take the entrepreneur route. Not everything we do we get right, particularly the first time around.

-A few will continue along as a small business, employing a handful of people, bringing in revenues of between US$50,000 and US$250,000 each year. Their spark will turn into a small fire, bringing warmth and comfort to those nearby. They include solar installation companies, farmer support programs, and female hygiene companies. These ventures are fantastic, and the world needs more of them.

-A smaller number will figure out a way of becoming a business that is on track to scalability and sustainability, where they will begin to reach hundreds or thousands of customers in a meaningful way and see their revenues kick past the US$250,000 mark. Their spark will turn into several fires, spreading out across their country and bringing warmth to many. We've seen these companies in the form of health clinics, small restaurant groups and education projects.

-And then, occasionally, some founders will grow a brilliant business. Their spark will turn into a wildfire that will spread quickly across an entire country. They will innovate highly scalable ideas, providing value to many people, and attract powerful partners that rapidly accelerate their growth. In our experience, these are online financial platforms, highly sophisticated education programs or school networks, or new health innovations tailored to an emerging market. These entrepreneurs bake scale into their model from the beginning and can't rest until they reach it.

The goal of this book is to try to help more entrepreneurs sit in this last set.

Through our formal ygap programs we are only able to reach the hundred or so businesses a year we mentioned earlier, but hopefully, this book is one way to reach more. While it would be nice to have you on one of our programs somewhere, we hope that if you are reading this, it will equip you with many of the skills that you will need to turn your early venture into something with real power, that makes change at scale. Indeed, let that be a challenge to you. We think that the following pages of this book will give you enough to create, launch, and grow your business. As the founder of Leapfrog Investments, Andy Kuper, once said to us: "End your apprenticeships, and get to work."

Is being an impact entrepreneur the best way to make change?

There are, of course, many ways to make change at scale in the world.

You could try to make a difference by running for public office. We certainly need more good people as politicians in a world where many struggle to trust our elected officials.

You could be an activist and, like the leaders behind Skolstrejk för Klimatet (School Strike for Climate) or Black Lives Matter, using social media, civil disobedience, and public actions to drive change.

You could begin a non-profit and fundraise for a cause you believe in.

While all these approaches are laudable, this book won't help you a whole lot with them.

Instead, this book is designed to help you build a business that makes a difference.

This doesn't imply that building a business is the best approach to make a difference in the world, or that it is more important or powerful than these other approaches.

It just means that it is what we know best, so it is what we can teach.

Many of the examples we provide will focus on the impact they have on people, as this has been the focus of the ventures we back. That said, there is nothing stopping you from having a different focus and goals, like helping the environment.

So, sticking to what we know, how will this book help you to build a business that will change lives for the better?

How will this book teach me to be an entrepreneur that changes lives?

As we move through the pages, we aim to help you learn how to build out your impact business in a few ways.

1. We will share with you all the practical tools we have learned as we've built, and helped others build, impact businesses. From the fun early moments of coming up with your company's name, to the stages of maturity that see you hiring the team that takes over from you one day.
2. We will also share stories about entrepreneurs we have worked with who have turned tiny ideas into powerful businesses that make huge impacts. You will hear real stories of their frustration, despair, success, breakthrough, and grit. Because business names change, businesses

come and go, and founders move onto new chapters, you'll often find that we haven't used their names in this book, as we'd prefer you to learn from their stories rather than get too excited about them as people.
3. We encourage you to move through the coming pages like it's a workbook. If you are reading this digitally, perhaps get yourself a notepad to write down ideas as you move along the pages. If you are reading a physical copy, consider using sticky notes here to keep your ideas together (so they can be updated as your ideas change). You can read it all in one go and come back to key points as they become more relevant; or you may decide to implement the steps as they come, using this book as a constant companion as you build your company. We love seeing copies of our book covered with the owners' writing and filled with sticky notes.

What is an impact entrepreneur?

The term entrepreneur gets thrown around rather liberally, yet it remains poorly understood by many people. So, we will break it down simply.

Let's say that there are five fish and chip shops on the main street of a small town in England. If a sixth person came along (let's call him Steven) and wanted to open another fish and chip shop on the main street, selling the same menu as the others, it would be a stretch to call them an entrepreneur. Instead, we would call them a small business owner, and probably one with a short-lived business at that.

An entrepreneur, however, (let's call her Mary) might realize that most people in the town eat their fish and chips on Friday nights, usually driving from the main street down to the beach with their hot parcels of food. Mary, the entrepreneur, might talk the lifeguards at the beach into using their building for five hours every Friday, and cooking up fish and chips to capture the Friday crowd. She might put on some live music from 5-7pm to attract even more people, and she will be sure to sell some drinks and ice creams to make even more money.

See, the entrepreneur (Mary) is not someone who simply opens a business; instead, they are looking at a market that is not working as well as it could and deciding to do things differently. Mary doesn't become yet another fish and chip shop owner like Steven on the main street; she offers something unique, and more than likely beats him and all the other competition too.

Now, the sad part of the story is that Mary could be so successful that she takes too many customers from the old fish and chip shops and forces them out of business. The economist Joseph Schumpeter would call her a "creative destroyer" and, in her own way, she would be disrupting an industry just like Henry Ford did for cars, before his company was disrupted again almost a hundred years later by Elon Musk's Tesla.

So, entrepreneurs change things. They break and remake markets. They put dents in economies and histories. Sometimes, they make things better, providing services that make us happier, healthier, or more connected. But, sometimes, entrepreneurs have negative impacts that might see them making the world less clean, less safe, or less prosperous.

We believe that in a world where trust for our politicians, bankers, and companies is so low, entrepreneurs have huge potential for good. We hope for entrepreneurs that don't spend all of their time sucking us into their addictive social networks, games, or online stores, but instead choose to direct their minds and hearts towards solving meaningful problems. We think the world needs entrepreneurs creating good jobs, building great schools, improving healthcare, and making communities safer and more equitable.

People like this have traditionally been called social entrepreneurs, and a whole sector has built up around this term. There are books written about social entrepreneurs, organizations like Ashoka dedicated to supporting them, and events like the Skoll World Forum where they gather. For years, though, we've seen plenty of entrepreneurs doing good things in the world who don't fit neatly into the "social entrepreneur" category. They've not won Ashoka fellowships, attended Skoll, and certainly haven't completed a log-frame analysis for their business.

But they are entrepreneurs that are changing lives.

So that's how we refer to them.

(Note: If you prefer to use the term "social entrepreneur," as many still do, that's fine too!)

I've already got a business idea; can I jump ahead?

We understand that each person reading this book is at a different point of their entrepreneurial journey.

You might have an idea that you are really excited about and are already convinced is going to be huge.

Or perhaps you are at an inflection point in your career, where you are tired of being an employee but don't yet know how to embark on life as your own boss.

Wherever you are, we are going to ask you to all start with us at the beginning, just for a few chapters. We work with many impact entrepreneurs each year, and as we move through the process laid out in this book, we find that at least a third of them pivot their ideas dramatically, another third make a bunch of small but important tweaks, and the final third remain convinced that they have the right idea (which they well might!).

So, are you sitting comfortably? Because, for the next hour or so at least, we are going to be looking at the EXPLORATORY phase.

This is when you are trying to identify the problem you think is worth solving, digging deep down to better understand it and inform what you think your best solution could be. So, it is a time for research, for understanding your potential customers, and for looking for the gap that has been missed by everyone else. If you do the exploratory phase well, you can leap into the next phase with confidence.

The next phase is a fun one (but also sometimes scary). In STARTUP, you really have one goal. And that is to find a repeatable, scalable, and sustainable model.

Repeatable means, if we did this on Tuesday and this thing happened, then if we do it again next Tuesday, we can expect a similar result. Scalable means that if you had the right resources (i.e., the right people, or machines, or warehouse, or website), you can expect to sell a lot more of the product you have created. Sustainable means that you make more money than you spend, and that you can create a team that can do this for years to come. During the startup phase, you need to operate as leanly as you can (meaning it doesn't cost a lot of money to run the business) in order to get to a proof point as quickly as you can. Sustainable also means that you can operate this business in a way that doesn't negatively impact people or the planet. Developing environmentally friendly, ethical, and equitable business practices will be something you continue to do over the course of your journey as an entrepreneur, but the best place to start thinking about this is in the startup phase. There is no use launching an impact business that improves lives in one area but makes them worse in another.

If you make it through that stage, then you move into GROWTH, which is where you actually build out the team, company, and infrastructure that you need to get your product to as many people as makes sense.

Then, following years of this hard work, some companies make it through to MATURITY, where your little idea has gone all the way to changing the system. By this point, plenty of people are trying to copy you, you have grown well beyond your original market, and you have built an empire.

But, we have got ahead of ourselves. As exciting as all of this sounds, remember that we are all going to go back to exploratory for a little bit, because if we get things right in exploratory, we can save ourselves years of work, a lot of money, and significantly reduce the risk that we totally fail and have to give up.

Can your swimming instructors swim?

If you are trying to start a business, there is a long list of hackathons, bootcamps, accelerators, incubators, meetups, online courses, and university degrees you can sign up for.

Before you spend any more time and money investing in some or many of these (as plenty of startup entrepreneurs do), ask yourself an important question: Can your swimming instructors swim?

Say you decide that you want to learn how to swim.

You go online and find a nice-looking website promising a great swimming course in your neighborhood. You sign up and head along a few weeks later to the class, stepping into a room with some tables and chairs and a curious lack of a really important feature: a swimming pool. Your instructor begins moving through a slide deck, gives you a nice template explaining some of the strokes, shows you a video of the great American swimmer Michael Phelps winning a gold medal in the 100-meter freestyle, and then wishes you luck in your swimming endeavors. After the class, when you ask your instructor a few questions, they refer you back to the templates and the PowerPoint slide deck, and then admit that they haven't done a whole lot of swimming themselves, but that they did the same course the year before. You head on home, still curious about swimming, but with very little to help you stay afloat when you next jump into the water.

You keep looking, and continue dreaming of the moment when you will be able to swim as well.

Then imagine that, one day, you enroll in another class, and when you turn up for day one, you realize your instructors can swim. In fact, they have been swimming for years. They quickly run you through the basics, but then they do something really important. They have you get in the pool. You start in the shallow end, with them supporting you, and then as your confidence grows you move into the deeper parts. It isn't easy, and as you go above your height you swallow a bit of water, and sometimes it feels scary; but, ultimately, well, you start to figure it out. Your instructor is there and can help you if you are really sinking, but they know that you will learn quicker the less they hold onto you. They can share some tips with you, but you will choose what feels right and decide which of them you want to take on board.

So, in this book, can your swimming instructors swim? As your authors, do we know what it takes to be an entrepreneur that changes lives?

First, we use examples of the best entrepreneurs we have worked alongside over the last decade. Their insights are scattered throughout the book, and you can draw lessons from where they succeeded, and also from the moments where they failed.

We also bring our own hard-earned experience in launching businesses and organizations that make a difference in the world.

After years working in social impact projects in East Africa, in 2010 we co-founded an organization that is now known as ygap.org. We work across the world raising millions of dollars each year to catalyze innovative solutions to poverty and inequality. ygap is an impact accelerator, meaning we identify early-stage impact entrepreneurs across Africa, Asia, and the Pacific and we invest in their ideas. Entrepreneurs that we have backed have gone on to impact more than a million people through creating jobs, improving homes, or providing quality healthcare or education. Throughout the ygap journey, we have had to figure out how to run teams, raise money, move through mergers and acquisitions, balance budgets, sell products, work with co-founders, build brands, and juggle the many other challenges of running a social enterprise.

I (Aaron) am also a co-founder of Education Changemakers (EC). EC works across the globe to improve education systems, has some of the world's largest technology companies as our clients and works with a great deal of educators each year.

After 10 years of growth, this company was acquired by the technology unicorn Go1.

We have seven degrees between us in economics, community development, international politics, strategy, and education from universities including Cambridge. We have run orphanages, community projects, and schools in some of the world's most challenging communities. We have worked closely with more than a thousand impact startups and been investors in more than 50 of them. We have merged organizations, been acquired, acquired others, founded a bunch that haven't worked, and provided consulting support to major companies like Microsoft and Apple, governments, and leading humanitarian agencies. We started our first companies and organizations with nothing in the bank, spending the first few years juggling night shifts as bartenders and nannies to pay our bills, so we know well the terror and joy of startup.

Now we live with our two boys, Finn and Atlas, by the beach in Australia, so to loop back to the little metaphor, we swim quite a lot these days.

Let's jump in the water together.

It's worth noting …

It's important also for us both to also acknowledge how lucky we've been.

We both grew up in good families who worked hard to put food on the table and put us through school.

We were both lucky enough to get into good universities.

We have had plenty of doors opened to us along the way due to privileges that we know exist.

We also know that many entrepreneurs around the world aren't quite as lucky as us. It's why we co-founded ygap, to try to help democratize entrepreneurship. But, we also know that some of the approaches we cover in this book won't be as easy to implement for everyone. We've tried our best to differentiate for different markets, but where we get that wrong we apologize.

We also developed many of these ideas during a particular era, so some of concepts may be outdated by the time you read this. We encourage you to take what you can and update or adapt when needed to suit your company's circumstances.

Finally, before we jump in, Kaitlin wanted to make it clear that while we both have our names on this book, I (Aaron) am the writer and brought the words together for this book. But I wanted to make it clear that the ideas that fill the book have been a collaborative effort between the two of us over the last decade, galvanized through experiences we've shared and debated and refined together many times.

Is being an impact entrepreneur right for you?

Let's say you want to make some money.

You come up with an idea to sell funny T-shirts, with cheeky slogans on them.

You get them printed in Bangladesh at the factory that offers you the cheapest price on Alibaba.com, have them sent to you in a shipping container by sea, where you then sell them through a website you built in Squarespace. Seems like a simple enough idea.

Chances are, though, there are already a bunch of websites selling funny T-shirts, and you will need to compete with them somehow. There are a few levers that you could pull to stand out from your funny T-shirt competitors. These could include making your T-shirts cheaper, making your website more appealing, paying for more online marketing, or striving to making your T-shirts funnier than the others.

Now let's say you change your mind before you start and want to make a difference with your T-shirt company, rather than just making money. What are some ways that you could do this?

-Rather than being funny, your messages could have a social mission instead, but you run the risk of reducing your customer base.

-You might commit to sourcing your T-shirts from a factory that provides awesome working conditions for its staff, but the chances are if you do this, your T-shirts are going to be far more expensive than your competitors.

-You might commit to trying to help the environment, but then unfortunately, your idea to sell cheap funny T-shirts suddenly doesn't seem very eco-friendly.

As you can see, the easier thing to do is to forget your social conscience and just sell as many cheap T-shirts as you can, faster than your competitors. You will need to forget about the working conditions in the Bangladeshi factory, and the fact that 4,000 liters of water is used to make the cotton for one T-shirt. But hey, if you can forget about all of this, you might make a buck or two with your idea!

However, maybe you are the kind of entrepreneur who finds it hard to simply "make a buck." Maybe you do care about the lives of the people in the factory in Bangladesh. Or the 4,000 liters of water. If so, maybe impact entrepreneurship IS for you.

Five more reasons not to be an impact entrepreneur

If you finished the last page and thought, *YES! I am an impact entrepreneur*, we want to challenge your thinking a bit more.

Let's push the romance of being an impact entrepreneur aside for a moment and lean into just five of the many reasons why this might not be the right life choice for you.

1. You probably won't have a regular paycheck for a couple of years. You will have to pay other people every month, but often you will go without. This means when your rent is due, you might have to scramble to pay it. It might mean you can't afford to eat out with your friends every weekend or go on that vacation you keep seeing everyone post about on Instagram. Having very little personal money is particularly hard if you have kids, family members that depend on you, or you have a whole bunch of debt hanging over you. If you like money a lot, the safest route (at least in the short to medium term) is staying as an employee in someone else's business.

2. Professionally, you'll think of almost nothing else for at least seven years. We have met plenty of entrepreneurs who think that they can get their idea going quickly, make a bunch of cash, hire a team, and then retire early. But, in our experience, and from what we have seen from the many startups we've worked with or those that we have launched and exited ourselves, it takes around seven years of hard work and hustle to make a business a success (and, of course, even then it's never guaranteed). That is a bunch of years in startup, bootstrapping the company to stay alive, then a few years of building out the team to move into growth, then a few years trying to make the growth strategy work. The likelihood is that it usually takes more than seven years, but that's the minimum you need to commit to. If you can't realistically buckle in for at least those first seven, this is probably a good moment to reconsider if this is really for you.

3. You probably won't get rich from doing this. As an impact entrepreneur, there is a good chance you won't get the big pay day that more deliberate, business-focused entrepreneurs might achieve. What we mean here is that it is easier to make a bunch of cash through an "exit" (where people buy your company off you) if you are just a money-making machine. If you are trying to make a difference and make money, you are far less attractive to private equity buyers, or even the stock market. Now, this is already changing, and there are certainly some examples of impact entrepreneurs who have done very well financially (power to them), but right now, this is the unfortunate reality you will most likely face.

4. As a boss, even of an impact business with all these great social change vibes, there are times that people in your team won't like you. It doesn't matter how nice you are to them, or how positive the culture is in your company, you are going to have to make tough calls which have real impacts on people's lives and opinion of you. Even though you are coming to work each day to make a difference, sometimes it will feel like the biggest problems you face in a day will be from the humans that are part of your team.

5. Being a founder comes with stress. You will have sleepless nights thinking about how to balance the budget, where you are going to find money, new products that are not working, or how you are managing your staff. It comes with the job. Being an entrepreneur, let alone an impact entrepreneur, is stressful stuff.

Still with us?

Despite some of the challenges we've just touched on, we absolutely think you should do this. Here are five reasons why.

1. **You will be your own boss.** Which is awesome. That means you don't need to interview ever again for a job. You are no longer a job taker but a job maker. It also

means you don't need any of those awkward growth meetings with your manager where you set KPIs and have them analyze your performance – you just set your own targets now (but that might come from your board if you get to the point where you need one). You don't have to squirm while you ask for a pay rise – you just decide what you can pay yourself from your own company. You don't have to ask for time off – you just take it. Welcome to a world of freedom.

2. **You have the power to put things right.** If you work for a company, there are plenty of people to blame for things not working. Maybe management is bad, or your suppliers are slow, or your competitors are outspending you, or people just don't like your product anymore. As an entrepreneur, the person to blame if things aren't working is you. It is your responsibility to improve the product, or market better, or hire better people. While this can be terrifying, the intellectual challenge of knowing that your destiny lies in your hands is a pretty electrifying way to live.

3. **You will go to bed each night knowing that you are making a difference, and there are few better feelings in the world.** While comparing yourself with others isn't a healthy way to live, the next time you are at a party and people around the circle are explaining what they do, it's a nice feeling to know that you are making the world better rather than auditing a boring company's financials or selling something you don't believe in.

4. **You have the freedom to build what you want to build.** The decisions are yours. What the brand looks like, how to spend your profits, what strategies to go after. You are literally making decisions all the time, and living with that autonomy is exciting.

5. **Every now and then you will cry happy tears.** Through all the years of working and the scariest of moments, sometimes you will take a moment to reflect on the life you have helped to change that day, and it will all be worth it.

    So with all that covered, let's get to work.

Chapter 1

In 2007 we sold most of what we owned, handed back the keys to our rented apartment in Sydney, Australia, and took a one-way flight to East Africa. In the years before this, while I was an officer in the military and Kaitlin was studying education,

CHAPTER 1

we had dreamed of trying to make a difference for people living in extreme poverty. We spent our first three months in Kenya, living through the post-election period which saw some of the worst violence the country has seen in decades, and then moved to Tanzania to help lead a secondary school for kids in a challenging township north of Dar es Salaam.

We quickly settled into the township that was to be our new home and got to work. Every morning we would wake up with smiles on our faces, make a cup of strong black coffee, blast our cheap little radio with local tunes, and get fired up for a day trying to bring change to the lives of a group of kids who really needed some positive breaks to come their way.

We set some big goals – the biggest being getting at least 10 of the older kids through the national exams and on the road to university. In a school where only one student had achieved this in the three previous years, the odds were against us. An already tough job was made even tougher in the first six months, with each of us suffering five bouts of malaria; and being subject to investigations from the police (who suspected we were CIA), curses from local witch-doctors, and even a handful of pretty serious death threats.

My parents came to visit the school when we had been there for almost a year and, when they saw how we were living, they sat us down and told us how worried they were that we were going to die in the township. My parents are passionate, compassionate, and well-traveled people, but they found it hard to understand why we were pushing so hard to meet the goals we'd set.

But we knew our why.

We loved the kids in the school. They were our why. When we first moved to the township, we were shocked by the estimation that two in five people were HIV positive and that four in five kids didn't finish high school. We felt that the school could be a beacon of hope in the community and were desperate to do what we could to try to make sure that hope was realized. So, we fought for it with everything we had.

We love this line from Friedrich Nietzsche: "The one who has a why to live by can bear almost any how." It means that if you know why you are doing what you're doing – why you're getting up each day and going back in to fight for something – you can get over all the barriers that come your way. And as an impact entrepreneur there will definitely be barriers. We've seen entrepreneurs we work with continuing while gang violence explodes around them, and others restaff their teams after their best people have tragically died during a global pandemic. The common link we see each time they push through struggles is their passion to solve the problem they've identified. Indeed, hardship doesn't break them; it galvanizes them.

We often say that "your why should make you cry." You should care so much about what you are fighting for that, when you take a moment to reflect on it, and think about the people you are serving and the future you hope for, it brings tears to your eyes. Later in the book we will check back in with our story to see if our "why" was strong enough to help us figure out the "how" of leading change in this particular community. But for now, let's focus back on you.

Do you know your why? Do you have something that deeply moves you, that makes you so sad, or angry, or frustrated that it wells up emotion deep inside of you?

Start your impact entrepreneurship journey with a clear idea of what you are most passionate about.

CHAPTER 1

Check-in

OK. Before you power ahead and just keep reading on, it's worth checking in on this question we just posed to you. Chances are that when we asked you if you knew your why, you are one of two types of people:

Person 1: As soon as we asked you what your why was, you knew straight away. The challenge that you are most passionate about, be it refugees, or women, or children, immediately popped into your head. If that is you, awesome! We'd encourage you to keep powering through the next few pages to get even more clarity and focus about the difference you want to make in the world.

Person 2: You really struggled on that last page. You don't really know what your why is. If this is you, don't stress. Trust the process that is ahead of you in this book, because experience shows us that the chances are in just a few pages you are going to start to feel a lot more like Person 1.

Let's get back to it.

Finding your why

Your life's purpose.

Pretty big question, isn't it?

But it is one that we think about a lot. What is a life well lived? What is the kind of life that you can look back on and think,

Well, that was really something?

Over the years, we've developed a little theory on this, and boiled it down to three things:

1. Love: Did you give and receive great love in your life?

2. Life: Do you enjoy life? Did you have moments of great joy, excitement, sadness, inspiration, and curiosity?

3. Legacy: Did you make a difference beyond yourself? Was the world better because you lived?

These are big ideas to be thinking about and are perhaps not something you can pin down just by reading this page. But by leaning into our passions and trying to make a positive difference on a problem we care about, we've experienced all three of these.

So how do you identify a particular problem you want to solve? For us, and for many of the impact entrepreneurs we have worked with, there are two major things that we see over and over.

The first is a lived experience of the problem you want to solve.

Like a founder of health clinics in Kenya who became inspired to do his work after the preventable death of his uncle.

Or the founder of an infant mortality organization who grew up with the trauma of knowing his twin brother had died in childbirth.

Or the founders of an insurance company who watched their family lose their home after a medical emergency put a strain on their family budget.

The second is that there is a problem that just breaks your heart, and you struggle to think about much else. It completely consumes your thinking. This one is easy to identify. It is where a specific challenge in the world takes up a huge amount of space in your head and heart, and you find it difficult to think about much else in your day. Greta Thunberg, the climate change activist, is of course a powerful example of this. She is living through a period of severe climate change, so she has lived experience, but it is also clear that she is absolutely consumed by the change she feels is needed for the environment. You can see the passion, and even the rage, oozing out of her every time she stands up and speaks. Just watch a video of her speaking at any event she attends. As she grew up, she was not thinking about the grades she would get in school, or what she would study in university in a few years; instead, she has been totally focused on doing what she can to drive governments and people to do better for the environment.

Again, we have met plenty of entrepreneurs who think like this.

One entrepreneur is obsessed with mangoes and will skillfully steer almost any conversation he is part of towards his favorite fruit and the impact it can make in the world.

Another is consumed by clean water, and, since she was young, she has been fashioning filters from buckets left around her house.

Two math teachers we know who launched an education company spend their days and nights (you can tell by the black bags under their eyes!) completely focused on how to help children around the world fall in love with mathematics like they have.

What are the issues in the world that break your heart?

CHAPTER 1

Your why should make you cry

Have a moan

We want you to write down all the issues in the world that move you. We call this little activity "moaning minutes," and it is pretty simple.

You can either do it quickly (where you set a 10-minute timer for some concentrated complaining about all the horrible things happening in the world), or you can stretch out the complaining over a couple of weeks and just keep track of the things that upset you as you come across them by reading the news, observing the world around you, or when doing some soul searching. Get yourself a packet of sticky notes, or keep track in this book if you have a physical copy, and list all the challenges in the world that frustrate you, make you upset, or that you would like to be part of solving. Don't stop until you have at least 20.

Some examples might be (and these are all things that have been written down by entrepreneurs we have worked with):
- People are dying from preventable diseases.
- Refugees and asylum seekers are finding it hard to fit into society.
- Many young mothers die during childbirth.
- Students are not succeeding in school.
- People do not have access to electricity.

Build out your catalog of issues in the world (remember, you can do this quickly or over a few weeks), and when you have 20, you are ready to move on.

CHAPTER 1

1. _____
2. _____
3. _____
4. _____
5. _____
6. _____
7. _____
8. _____
9. _____
10. _____
11. _____
12. _____
13. _____
14. _____
15. _____
16. _____
17. _____
18. _____
19. _____
20. _____

(We acknowledge that this might feel crass, and it can feel like you are minimizing the real hardship of these issues by putting them into a list. So be sure to treat these issues with respect;

these are real problems facing real people. As you think about them, take a moment to think about how lucky you may have been in your life.)

Choose one issue

We just had you list a whole bunch of problems in the world that upset you. You might have written them down in five rage-soaked minutes, or it might have been something that you brought together over a few weeks.

Your job now is to look at that list and pick just one problem.

A word of warning, though …

You are going to try to create a company to solve the issue you pick.

It should be something you are willing to dedicate the next decade of your life to.

It's an important decision.

Once we've decided the issue we want to help solve, we precede it with "*it is unacceptable that …*"

Over the years we have seen thousands of these written out by entrepreneurs, and some that stick out to us are:

- *It is unacceptable that* skilled workers in our city cannot find work.

CHAPTER 1

Or ...

- *It is unacceptable that* many women who leave prison return within a few years.

Or ...

- *It is unacceptable that* children at my local school are going hungry.

Once you have your "*it is unacceptable that*" statement, jot it down here if you have a physical book, or as a comment if you are reading digitally. (It doesn't have to be perfectly worded just yet; it can be simple and raw).

It is unacceptable that ...

_____
_____
_____

Don't think about solutions yet

It's natural to jump straight away into thinking about solutions.

As you wrote down your "*it is unacceptable that*" statement, you might have started to think, *I could do this*, and raced into fleshing out an idea.

Don't. Well, not yet.

Instead, we need to spend some more time trying to better understand the problem we have identified.

And if you are reading this book with an idea already in mind, again we ask you to put it to the side for the next few chapters (we are going to help you make it even better if you trust the process). All you need right now is that phrase "*it is unacceptable that.*" And with just those few crucial words, we are done with step one in the journey.

Your journey to becoming an entrepreneur that changes lives

We've got a bunch of steps ahead of us, but for now, well done, that's step one done!

CHAPTER 1

1. It is unacceptable that ✓

Chapter 2

CHAPTER 2

We believe ...

What future are you fighting for?

All being well, you'll be old one day.

You will have wrinkles in strange places and hair in even stranger places.

And, hopefully, you can look back on your life and think, *Wow, we really did something there.*

Think of what it would feel like to be an old Nelson Mandela, looking back with pride on a lifetime of incredible struggle, knowing that you were a key player in changing the history of an entire country.

Rosa Parks would have felt the same, knowing that her actions on a bus all those years ago shifted the lives of millions.

As would Jonas Salk, who invented the polio vaccine and saved and improved the lives of countless people.

At this point of the process, we want you to think this big. Not for the accolades and fame, but for that feeling of knowing you did something powerful for the world.

We think the easiest way to do this is to simply flip your "*it is unacceptable that*" statement into a "*we believe*" statement. So, for example ...

It is unacceptable that skilled workers in our city cannot find work.

CHAPTER 2

Becomes ...

We believe in a Dhaka where all skilled workers can find a good job.

Or ...

It is unacceptable that many women who leave prison return within a few years.

Becomes ...

We believe in a Uganda where all women who leave prison never find themselves behind bars again.

The scale of your ambition is up to you. Do you want to change the world, your country, a region? Some people say, "We believe in a world where ..." Others say, "We believe in a Canada where ..." Others say, "We believe in a Soweto where ..." While the scope of your sentence depends on the kind of change you want to see, we would encourage you to think big. Indeed, if your idea is not going to change a million lives, then we'd challenge you to rethink it.

It's also worth noting that you are not single-handedly going to make this change a reality. Instead, you will be part of a movement of many people who strive to bring it to fruition.

So, you need to think how big you want to go, in your lifetime, and you need to flip your "*it is unacceptable that*" statement into something far more positive with a "*we believe*" sentence.

Write down your "*we believe*" sentence here, either in the book or digitally. You may even consider using a sticky note in your physical book, as this sentence may change over time. Also, the reason that we use the word "we" here is that we are implying right from the get-go that you are building a big idea, rather than trying to be the hero and go alone!

We believe in a _____ where ...
_____
_____
_____

And that is all you need for this stage of the process. While all we did was create a short sentence in this chapter, (that might just define the rest of your life). Step two done!

1. It is unacceptable that ✓
2. We believe ✓

Chapter 3

CHAPTER 3

But right now the reality is ...

Time to get the facts

There is an old saying that goes 'if we have data, let's look at data. If all we have are opinions, let's go with mine'.

It's a useful way to think.

So, let's look at some numbers. At this stage of your entrepreneurship journey, opinions are nice to have, but you really need strong data to back up your hunches. Opinions are easy to throw out there, and we are sure you have heard a bunch over the years from opinionated taxi drivers, your uncle who listens to too much talk-back radio, or people who share a little too freely on social media.

So don't be that person.

Instead, be the entrepreneur who can talk about an issue in the world, and very quickly back it up with powerful sets of data.

This means you need to do some research to back up your "*it is unacceptable that*" and "*we believe*" statements. Search high and low for some irrefutable data to prove that the problem is real, compelling, and worth solving. Make sure that the places you are getting the data from are reputable, so look for United Nations reports, statistics from the government of the country you are looking to work in (if you deem them reputable), or reports from major non-profits.

And when you find statistics, humanize them. Saying "one in every three people" creates more empathy than "36.2% of the population ..." Or try to paint a picture by saying things like, "Imagine a classroom of 30 children; now, take a moment to think about the fact that currently 10 of those children are suffering from ..."

Search far and wide for good data, but then choose the top two statistics that really stick out to you. And then finish the sentence "*but right now, the reality is that*" with them. You will use these over and over as you develop your strategy, pitch your idea, and grow your company, so make them good!

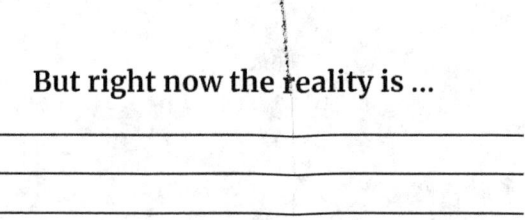

But right now the reality is ...

_____

_____

_____

And with that, step three is done! You are powering through!

1. It is unacceptable that ✓
2. We believe ✓
3. But right now the reality is that ✓

Chapter 4

The root cause we are going to focus on is ...

CHAPTER 4

It's complex

The problem that you've been thinking about over the last few chapters might seem rather simple at first, but the likelihood is that it is rather complex.

As an example, when we lived in Makuyu village in the Central Highlands of Kenya, an entrenched problem was children were dropping out of school. To show the complexity of poverty typical in the area, let's talk through a hypothetical situation.

Meet Margaret. She has two children, Mary, aged 14, and James, aged nine. To support the family budget, Margaret buys spinach at the Thika central market early each morning, and then returns home to sell this in the smaller Pundamilia village market in the evenings, making a profit of just over US$1 on a good day. She has plenty of bad days because often she cannot purchase high quality spinach, the prices at the central market fluctuate, or some evenings it seems that people just don't want to buy. She has a small one-acre farm where she grows her own maize and has two harvests each year. She often complains of feeling tired, but the local clinic has not been able to diagnose anything specific, and when she purchased malaria treatment tablets, she wasn't convinced that they were authentic. When she cannot travel to the market to purchase spinach because she is unwell, Mary does this for her, skipping school for the day. The father in the family, Joseph, passed away two years earlier, and it was said that he died from "pressure" (a more specific medical reason wasn't given). James has had recurring chest infections over the last two years, and while Margaret has tried a number of different antibiotics for him, nothing seems to have fixed his nasty cough. Buying these drugs is putting stress on the family budget, and recently Margaret has struggled to pay school fees for her children and purchase their school supplies even though they are largely subsidized by the government. Mary finds school boring but loves to read books and has many friends in her grade seven class. She also often feels tired, lives on a diet of maize flour and spinach, and drinks unfiltered water from the river. She attended a weekend computer training program run by a group from the United States which she enjoyed but has been unable to access a computer since the course. The family lives in a one-bedroom shack in the village near a popular bar, so everyone struggles to sleep at night when the bar is busy. Margaret is thinking of moving to Nairobi as her aunty has a shack in the city's Kibera slum and has offered a small room to the family.

So yes, with all this going on, Mary is at risk of dropping out of school.

But as you can see, the reasons why she might drop out are very, very complex and challenging. A broad category of "children dropping out of school" fails to account for such nuance and complexity.

What we need to attempt to do is to dig down further to understand Mary's realities. A powerful way to do this is by using a "root cause" tree tool.

What you need to do now (and please do this, don't just skim over this important step!) is to get yourself a piece of paper and draw a tree that looks a little something like this:

CHAPTER 4

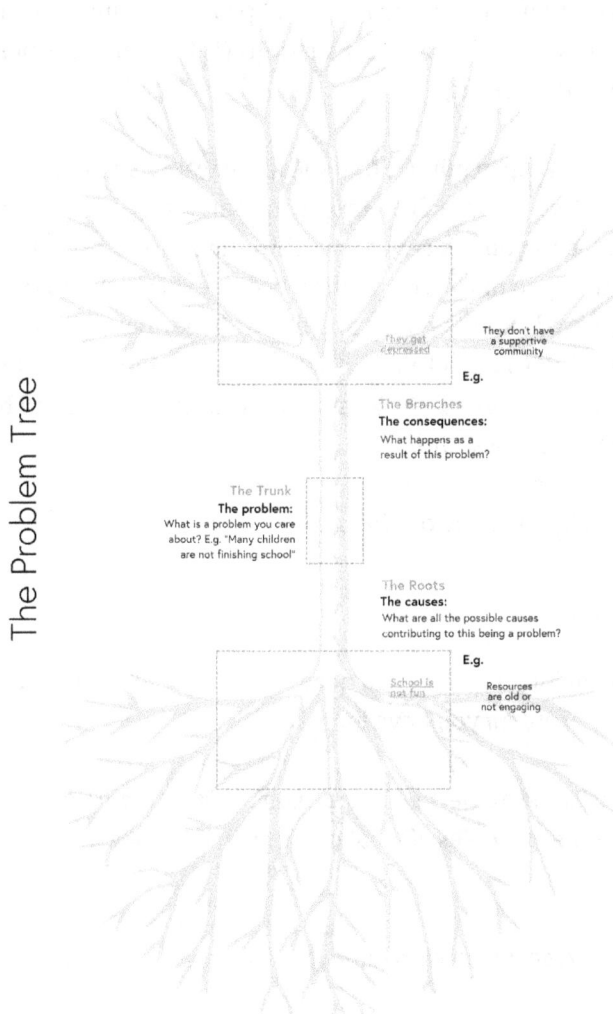

We will now go through how to use this tree you have drawn step by step, and we would encourage you to move through it carefully with us, as we often find that people who jump ahead without following the clear instructions (is that you?), almost always get this wrong!

One thing to keep in mind is that these root cause analysis trees are most effective when you take a good amount of time to fill them out, and you are actually within the community where you are trying to make a difference, because then you can truly get a sense of what is going on. If that is not possible, then you are going to need to make some assumptions here (and part of your time in the exploratory and startup phases will be validating these assumptions).

Let's start by focusing on the trunk.

The trunk

In the trunk of your tree, you need to simply and clearly state the broad problem you have identified.

Revisiting some of the "*it is unacceptable that*" statements from earlier, some examples of what could go in the trunk of the tree are:

- Skilled workers in our city cannot find work.

Or ...

- Many women who leave prison return within a few years.

Or ...

CHAPTER 4

– *Children at my local school are going hungry.*

Are you clear on your "*it is unacceptable that*" statement?

We are going to continue with our example, and, as you can see below, have written in the trunk of our tree that "many children are not finishing school."

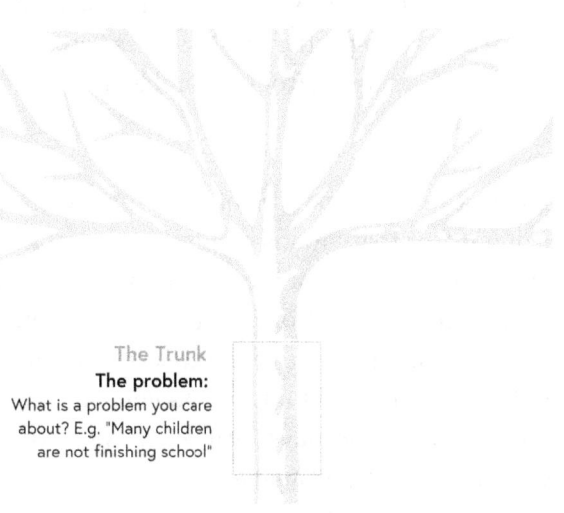

The Trunk
The problem:
What is a problem you care about? E.g. "Many children are not finishing school"

Remember, this is the problem you want to solve with your business, the one you wrote about in your "*it is unacceptable that*" statement and researched in your "*but right now, the reality is that*" statement. Keep it nice and simple; it is fine to be broad at this stage.

The big branches

Now that the trunk is filled in, you want to look up, at the branches. (If you are not filling out a tree on a page, we recommend, just one more time, that you take the time to do this rather than just reading ahead!)

The branches are where you detail the consequences of the problem in the trunk of your tree. Just to make sure you are totally clear (because this is where we sometimes see people go wrong), we are looking at the consequences here, which are the results that are emerging from the problem in the trunk of your tree.

If we consider the consequences of the problem we had in the trunk of our tree that "many children were not finishing school," they may include an increased number of teenage pregnancies, a greater level of frustration in teachers, depression among young people, or a reduction in the overall education levels in the community. As you can see on the branches of our tree, we have written these into the big branches, using very simple language.

CHAPTER 4

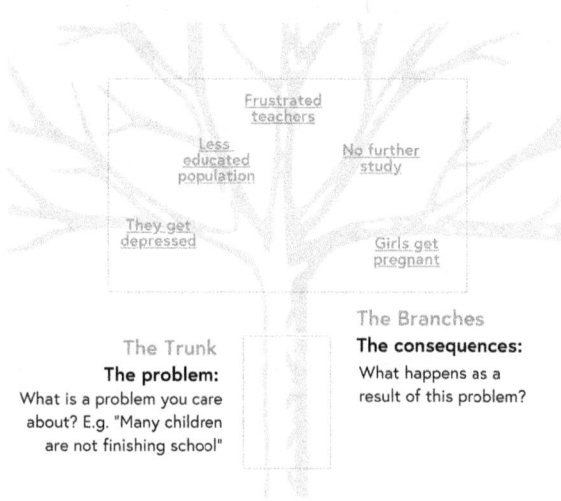

Following our example, consider your root cause tree.

Think of the first five consequences of the problem you have put into the trunk of your tree, and write them into the big branches.

The extended branches

Now, from the initial five major consequences, we continue to go up, asking ourselves, *And then what happens?*

To revisit our example of "many children are not finishing school," you can see on our tree that we have been able to list five main consequences we saw arising from the trunk. But then, for each of the consequences we asked, "and then what happens?," to fill out our tree even further. You can see that we were able to identify plenty of different consequences coming from the five branches, giving us a much richer understanding of the scope of the problem we are trying to solve, the complexity associated with it, and the knock-on effects.

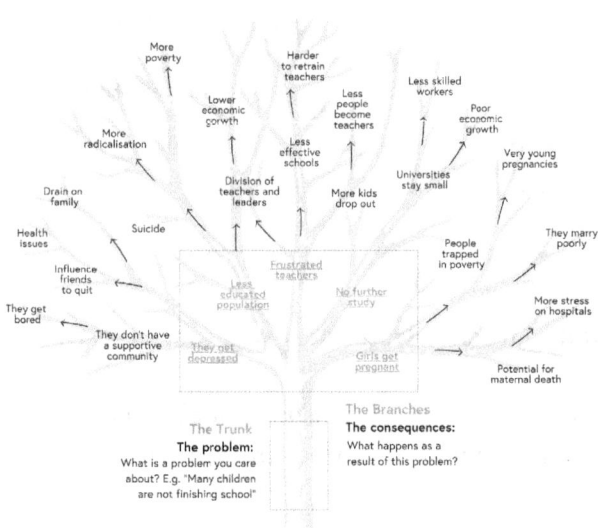

Why bother with the branches?

Getting our head around the consequences of the problem in the trunk of the tree help us to see all the reasons why we should work on a problem. Sometimes, to be honest, we discover that there are not many consequences, at which point we ask ourselves whether in fact it is an issue worth solving!

The other things to consider with these consequences is that everyone has their branch that concerns them. Maybe there is a big group of investors who are inspired to make a difference for women. Maybe a privileged school group that you are trying to mobilize behind your idea might be passionate about climate change. You might find that the local politician who you are trying to get on board is actually a big fan of solar energy. Throughout your journey as an entrepreneur you can use the consequences you have identified in your tree to find wins for others and get them on board with the cause you are fighting for.

There is another major reason why we spend time looking at the consequences.

Think of what happens when you trim the branches of a tree (that is, attack the consequences).

It grows back. Usually stronger than ever. Which is not good.

Sometimes, as impact entrepreneurs, we can fall into the trap of just taking on the consequences, spending huge amounts of time, effort, and money and never truly getting to the root causes of an issue. Which is what we need to do. We need to get to the roots because they are what's sustaining this tree.

The root causes are why the problem continues to exist.

The main roots

Just like we did with the five main branches, when we go underground, we first look at the five main reasons why the problem keeps happening (write these into the five main roots of the tree).

You will see we have done this with our issue below. We felt that the root causes of our trunk problem (that many children are not finishing school) included teacher quality being low, parents withdrawing their children, and the simple fact that maybe the students are not finding school fun.

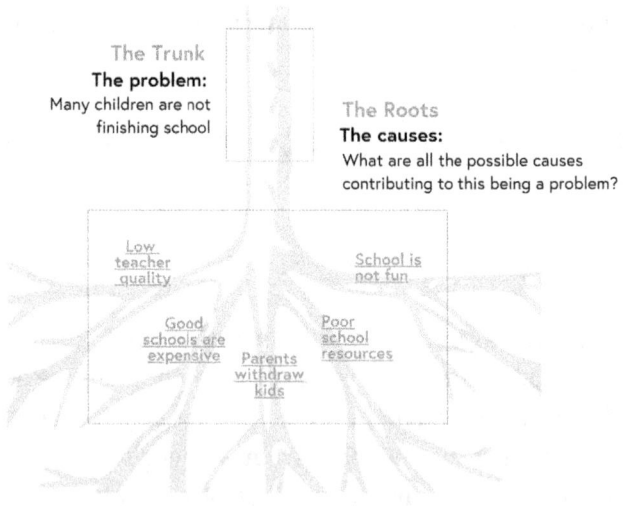

Jump back to your tree and write down what you think are the five main reasons why the problem in the trunk of your tree keeps happening. Remember, you can make assumptions around what you think the root causes are here, but if you really spend some time engaging with the community you are trying to help, you will be far better informed and perhaps more likely to find a killer solution.

The extended roots

Once you have your first five root causes down, you then want to expand out the roots. Keep asking "why does that happen" over and over. You can see from our example here we have gone two layers deep. If you are curious about this issue, go even further; the more insight you can gain, the more powerful your understanding of the problem in your trunk.

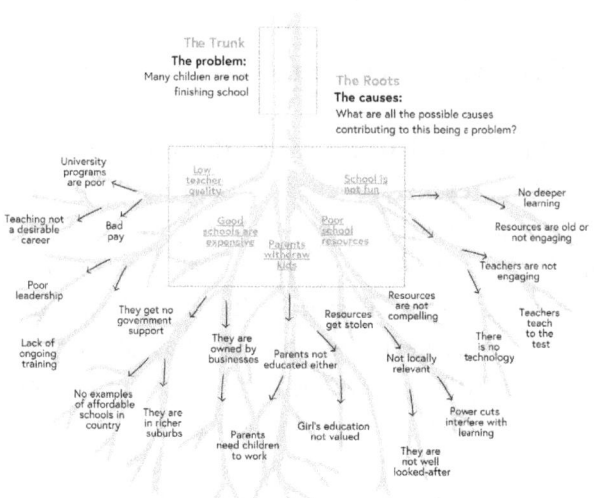

Picking just one root

A few years ago, we led an orphanage and community project in Makuyu, a small village in Kenya. While we were there, our team were trying to solve a whole raft of challenges in the community.

We did many of these root cause analysis trees during our time there, and indeed "many children are not finishing school" was one of them. Specifically, we were focused on the number of girls dropping out.

The consequences were heartbreaking, with far too many girls falling pregnant, contracting STIs (unfortunately, the village was near a truck stop with high levels of prostitution). The girls who were dropping out of school were trapped in poverty and, tragically, dying young.

These girls were our friends. It was heartbreaking.

For months we tried to understand this problem. We chatted with parents, teachers, teenage girls, their boyfriends, and anyone else we could think of to try to get a deeper understanding of what was going on. There were all sorts of root causes: the need for the girls to work on the family farm, the lack of educated female role models, the fact that for many students school was boring, and the feeling among some parents that they couldn't afford to invest in their girls.

One day we were chatting to a group of girls and I asked, "How many days a month do you usually miss?" When they became shy and one said timidly, "Around five," I decided to leave the conversation and let Kaitlin fully take over.

It turned out that every time they had their period (their monthly menstrual cycle), they skipped class.

While this problem is now commonly recognized in education in very poor communities (and we've seen countless sanitary pad programs since), back then, despite having several degrees in international development, it was the first that we had heard of this issue being so influential for the education of young girls. It also just wasn't a major issue in the kind of privileged, middle-class, safe communities where we had grown up in America and Australia. So when we looked at the root cause tree we had drawn up for girls dropping out of school, it was complex and ugly. There were a whole bunch of roots that were out of our control, and plenty more that we simply didn't have the resources to do anything about. But the issue of girls missing days of school each time their period came around was something we could try to focus on. And if we could keep the girls in school an extra four or five days a month, their chances of staying on at school might increase. As a result, we put a big circle around this root cause, and got to work trying to solve it.

Now imagine you take a step back and look at your tree.

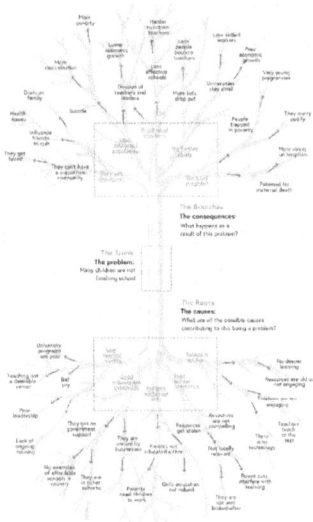

You hate that tree.

With the problem spray-painted on the trunk and all the horrible consequences on the branches, you really want this tree to die. (Stick with us on this metaphor – we don't usually like killing trees, just these bad ones!)

Again, don't fall into the trap of trying to snip away at the consequences (the branches) rather than getting down to the roots. This is almost always the wrong approach.

Now imagine that we invite a bunch of great people who are trying to solve this problem over to our backyard. They don't like this tree either. We give each of them a shovel and an axe. They look at all the root causes and start to decide which one they are most qualified (or most inspired) to chop through.

A smart impact entrepreneur would see at what roots other people are chopping, and then focus their efforts on the one being missed.

Every now and then you might help someone else on their root; but the reality is, the best job you can do is chop through the one root that you are focused on.

The refined and well-understood root cause you identify is the specific one that you are going to try to build a business to solve. To help you make your decision, ask yourself these questions:

1. What are you inspired to solve yourself? You should be excited by making a difference to the particular root cause you have identified.
2. What is in your control to solve? Think about whether it is realistic that you can actually solve some of these root problems. For example, if a school is a long way away from a major city, it is probably not in your control to pack it all up and move it into town!
3. Who else is already working on these roots? It is more than likely that there are good people out there already working hard on these roots, and we don't necessarily want to push them out of the way so we can get chopping on a root ourselves. As entrepreneurs, we like to be the "disruptors," but when you are talking about people's lives, you want to make sure that your disruption is a positive one! Take time to think about what is already happening and where the gaps are.

4. Will attacking that root be cost effective and have a big impact? This final question determines whether a viable business could be created, and whether any solution you come up with will put a dent into the problem.

As you can see in our example below, we've circled the root cause which speaks to the issue that 'good schools are expensive'.

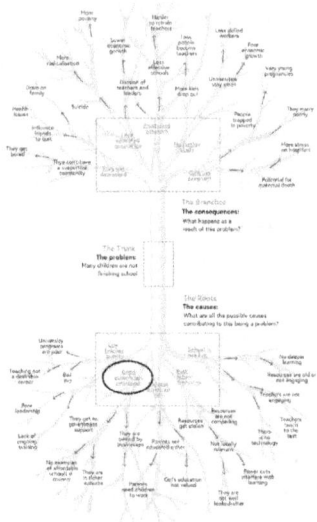

Take some time now to determine which root cause you would like to circle.

Once you have this determined, you are well on the part to

having a clearer understanding of the foundations of your business.

1. It is unacceptable that ✓
2. We believe ✓
3. But right now the reality is that ✓
4. The root cause we are going to focus on is ✓

Chapter 5

CHAPTER 5

Aha, time for ideas!

If you are thinking, *Now I can get back to my cool idea again and just move ahead with this*, we have some bad news for you. We are going to still ask you to park that one idea for little while longer while we help you come up with 49 more business ideas.

If you are thinking, *Wowzers, I don't even know where to start! How am I going to get to 50?!*, well, read on, friend. We are going to give you plenty of support to help you get to that number.

The first thing we need to do is come up with a "*how can we*" question.

Your "*how can we*" question will set the parameters for a design challenge for which you are now going to try to innovate 50 business ideas. It is really important that you create this question from the specific root cause you just circled (and not from the broader "*it is unacceptable that*" statement).

So, go back a few pages, remind yourself of the sentence where you wrote "the root cause we are trying to solve is …" and then flip that into a "*how can we*" question. Some examples that we have seen from other entrepreneurs have included:

How can we offer a high-quality schooling model for children in Nairobi at a rate that is half the price of similar schools?

Or

How can we reduce the significance of financial shocks for small-holding farmers?

Or

How can we improve the quality of health checks mothers receive in the last trimester of their pregnancy?

Now it's your turn! Write down your "*how can we*" question here. Make sure you are excited about it, because you are about to try to innovate 50 ideas to solve it!

(Note, if you are not excited about the "how can we" question you just came up with, take a step back and check that you circled the right root cause. If that doesn't work, step back again and figure out if you have the right "we believe" statement. If that doesn't work, you might need to do some soul searching and return to the first step and look at your "it is unacceptable that" statement. But hey, better to do that now rather than in five years when you realize you have spent a bunch of time working on something your heart isn't in!)

How can we ...

_____
_____
_____

Time to jump in at the deep end

Remember in the 'Can your swimming instructors swim?' section we said that we might push you into the deep end a little bit? Well, that starts now. Before we give you any innovation techniques, we want you to try to come up with at least 10 business ideas which answer your "*how can we*" question. Keep a list of them either here in this book, in a notebook, or on your device. Try your hardest to actually do this, and not just jump ahead to the next page. You won't build a great business just by reading this book, but you might build one by taking action!

1. _____
2. _____
3. _____
4. _____
5. _____
6. _____
7. _____
8. _____
9. _____
10. _____

CHAPTER 5

Now for some innovation tools

Hopefully you thrived when we pushed you into the deep end on the previous page, and were able to dream up at least 10 ideas to solve your "*how can we*" question! We are serious when we say that we want you to get to 50 different ideas, and now we are going to give you some tools, approaches, inspirations, and ideas to get this done. While you could just read through this book in one or two sittings, we really do recommend that you spend a few hours, or maybe some days over the coming month, to try to innovate these 50 ideas.

We'll start with five innovation rules you can keep in mind when you are trying to solve a "*how can we*" question.

While these rules can work well if you are innovating alone, they are most effective when you are doing this within a group of people. So perhaps think about bringing some creative people together, putting on some food and drinks for them, and then seeing how many ideas you can come up with together.

Also, when you use these rules, it can be helpful to explain them to the people you have brought together, and while this might sound funny, say out loud to the group, "Ideation rules are now in force."

And here they are:

Rule 1: Lots of ideas, please.

Don't hold back, keep the ideas coming thick and fast. It's why we keep throwing around that 50 number.

Why?

Because if you are going to spend the next seven years of your life on this, you want to make damn sure that it is a good idea! Also, in our experience, early ideas are rarely the ones that we actually end up pursuing and taking to scale. In fact, we quite like the line "first idea, worst idea," which helps us to park our initial thoughts and instead move ahead and really stretch our thinking.

There is some real proof that pushing out 50 ideas or more is a good use of your time. Our friends over at IDEO (a group of inventors and problem solvers) have been doing this for decades. Some professors tracked them over a series of projects that they were working on and found something really interesting. When they innovated 100 solutions to a problem, they found on average that ideas one to 60 produced a few interesting results. Ideas 61 to 80 often got a little crazy, as the team was pushing their creativity. But between ideas 81 and 100 there were often around six brilliant light-bulb moments that they wanted to move forward with. Their breakthrough innovations were coming during the final 20% of their brainstorm.

Let's play along with an example "*how can we*" question to

show you how we squeeze out as many ideas as possible. If you remember earlier when we were doing the root cause tree, we ended up circling "there are no examples of affordable, high-quality schools in our country." Therefore, the "*how can we*" question here would be "*how can we* provide examples of affordable, high-quality schools in our country?"

1. Let's launch our own affordable, high-quality school.
(Now that is pretty damn exciting, and you could very quickly get very inspired to build this school! But while it could be a great idea, you need to park it to one side, and try for 49 more).
2. We could record a documentary to profile affordable, high-quality schools in other places.
3. We launch a completely online school.
4. We could start a consulting company that goes into schools with a mission to halve their operating costs.
5. We could innovate a way to reduce the cost of building schools (the actual bricks and mortar).
6. We could come up with a way where you could have 100 students in a class but still get great learning.
7. We could train up parents and grandparents to be teachers and home school their students.

OK, so we are seven ideas in. Only 43 more to go. Easy!

Now onto the next innovation rule.

Rule 2: Crazy ideas are allowed (and encouraged)

This is really helpful because when we are in the early stages of innovating, we often put plenty of constraints on ourselves. We think about what we might be able to afford. Or what we might be able to do with our current knowledge and skills. And we need to step well beyond this. Because some ideas that are very normal now were crazy when people first suggested them.

For example, imagine a century and a half ago when Alexander Graham Bell was first telling people about the phone. Maybe his pitch went a little bit like this: *"If you talk into this receiver that is connected to another receiver, you can speak to each other even if you are not in the same room. And if we just connect every one of these receivers to every other receiver with millions of miles of cables over all the mountains of the world and under all the oceans, we will all be able to talk to each other whenever we want."* Might have seemed a little crazy, but, of course, the world did it.

When we innovate, we want to be open to any ideas, no matter how big or crazy they seem. For some inspiration, we were working with some 14-year-old students once and we asked them *"how can we ensure every child eats healthy food in the school?"* After hearing crazy ideas about air-dropped smoothies and swimming pools full of salad, one kid yelled, "Let's rip out all the trees and plant fruit trees!" If you walk around their school now, you can grab an apple straight from the tree. Pretty cool.

To model this, we will get crazy on our own question of *"how can we* provide examples of affordable, high-quality schools in our country?"

8. We could try to win the government contract to run every school in the country.

9. We could give the kids tapes to listen to in their sleep, so they learn that way.

10. We could have no teachers and instead the kids get paid to teach each other.

11. We could try to condense five years of high school into two years.

12. We could swap the school buildings for tents.

13. We could try to find a civilization of aliens in space and encourage them to come to Earth and be teachers in our school.

Yep, you read that right, we are thinking of training up aliens to be teachers. Crazy. But at least we are at 13 ideas now. Let's keep powering towards 50.

Rule 3: Yes, and ...

One of the reasons that we encourage lots of crazy ideas is that we don't know where they might go. They could be the catalyst for other ideas that might be great.

With this in mind, respond to any idea by saying, "*Yes, and ...*" – an idea that was made famous by the comic geniuses from Chicago's improv comedy team Second City. When you are innovating and see an opportunity to build on an idea, get into the habit of saying, "*Yes, and* we could also do ..."

For example, we could build on the craziest of our ideas so far, which has to be: "We could try to find a civilization of aliens in space and encourage them to come to Earth and be teachers in our school."

Using "*Yes, and ...*" we could add:

14. *Yes, and* we could also encourage great teachers from around the world to come and volunteer their services for free to keep the costs low.

Or ...

15. *Yes, and* we could program some awesome robot teachers to run brilliant lessons in our school.

Or ...

16. *Yes, and* we could find university students who have not been able to gain jobs yet to commit to being teachers for at least one year at our school.

OK, so we are getting somewhere. Only 34 more ideas to go. Easy, right?!

Rule 4: "We"

This is most powerful when done in a group. Quite simply, you need to use the word "we" a lot. If someone is concerned about one of the ideas, rather than shooting it down, they should say "we need to think about ..."

For example, if we think back to the idea of launching an online school, if you (or someone else in your innovation team) are worried about how strong the internet access is across the country, you wouldn't kill this idea by saying "people won't have good enough internet to access this online school." Instead, you would keep the innovation going by saying "we need to think about a way to make this online program accessible even if people have poor internet."

With this, the ideas flow again with ...
17. We could have a subscription service where the students receive a physical box of great learning every month.
18. They could pick up a pre-loaded tablet once a month with the next four weeks of learning programmed into it.
19. We could run a digital school during the day, and a cyber-café at night.
20. Could we run a school by SMS?

On we go to 50!

Rule 5: It's all good

You'll notice that we haven't shot down any of our ideas yet. We are at 20, and while we may have some inkling already about which of these ideas are the stronger ones, we withhold judgment. Importantly, as we power towards the magic 50, every idea is a good idea.

Therefore, if you are doing this in a group, it is important that no-one is negative about any ideas (or, to put it more positively, everyone thinks every idea is great!). Negativity can be expressed in so many ways, including seeing people:
- fold their arms;
- shake their heads;
- squish their faces up like they've just sucked on a lemon;
- mutter things under their breath;

- express their negative opinions out loud, saying things like "that will be too expensive" or "that has already been tried"; or

- try to come across as the smartest or most experienced person in the group and silence others.

We have all done some (or all) of these things, and while it can be hard to break these habits, enforcing these five rules is a great way to start. One handy tool we use when doing this as a team is to give a pen to someone who is feeling a little grumpy that day and ask them to write everyone's name in the team down on a piece of paper or whiteboard. If they spot anyone being negative, they put a mark next to that person's name, which equates to a small contribution to our Friday drinks fund. It pays to be positive in our team.

Your turn

To recap the five rules:

Rule 1: Lots of ideas, please

Rule 2: Crazy ideas are allowed (and encouraged)

Rule 3: Yes, and …

Rule 4. "We"

Rule 5: It's all good.

Now, equipped with these five innovation rules, it's time for you to go back to innovating more business ideas to answer your "*how can we*" question. You can do this by yourself or, if possible, get a team together to knock around some ideas. See if you can come up with at least 30 before you read ahead.

The different types of impact businesses you can create

Hopefully, you have now come up with at least 30 ideas for your "*how can we*" question, with the 10 you did on your own and the 20 more prompted by following our five rules (we got to 20 in that round, so you should be able to as well!).

It's time for another tool to help you get at least 10 more; the difference between profit and process impact businesses.

Let's start with the profit impact business, because it is the easiest to understand. Here you simply start a business that makes a profit. It can be anything you like; the goal is just to make a profit. Then you direct those profits to making an impact.

For example, using our "*how can we* provide examples of affordable, high-quality schools in our country" question, here are five more ideas:

21. Let's start a line of kids' books and donate profits to schools in need.
22. Let's start a line of children's lunchboxes and donate profits to schools in need.
23. Let's launch a line of healthy snacks for children and

donate profits to schools in need.

24. Let's start a school uniform company and donate profits to schools in need.

25. Let's start a summer camp program for children and donate profits to schools in need.

Pretty easy, isn't it?

All we are doing here is trying to run a business and, rather than trying to be the heroes ourselves and run the impact projects, we are simply giving this money to other people doing the impact work. It can be humbling, in a good way, to acknowledge that you don't have experience in education yourself and would prefer to invest money with the experts!

An example of a profit impact business is Newman's Own, started by the actor Paul Newman, who bottled up salad dressing (well at least he got someone to do it for him), sold a bunch of it, and donated all the profits to social missions (more than half a billion dollars so far, with the business thriving even after his death).

Now, a process impact business is a little more complex. This is where you still aim to make a profit, but with a specific mission for your business. For example, a company we were involved with for a number of years has a mission of trying to turn around the lives of drug addicts and gang members in Cape Town, South Africa. They run a furniture shop where the items are made by the men in their programs. The more furniture they sell, the more men they can help.

Another group, in Melbourne, Australia, has a mission to support refugees and asylum seekers. So, they run a cooking class and catering company, where all the chefs are newly-arrived refugees or asylum seekers. Again, the more events they run, the more refugees and asylum seekers they can help.

If we look at our example of "*how can we* provide examples of affordable, high-quality schools in our country," here are five possible innovations:

26. We could run a teacher training college, that charges fees to students or the local government, to supply schools with highly-qualified staff.

27. We could run an annual conference where we bring together the best schools in our country to share their ideas.

28. We could start a publishing company that prints "How to" guides with the best education approaches in our country.

29. We could start a travel company that specializes in providing field trips for excellent teachers from around the world to spend a term at schools in our country and have a great experience.

30. We could start a construction company that builds schools in an affordable way for clients.

With these new ways of thinking, try to come up with at least five profit business ideas and five process business ideas for your own "*how can we*" question.

Imitation is the sincerest form of flattery

Need another innovation tip to help you get to 50 business ideas?

This next one is pretty simple.

Copy things.

Or collaborate with people who are doing something that you think could work in your market.

There are plenty of companies in the world who have seen what a company is doing and have decided to do something similar. For example, there is more than one company in the world manufacturing cars, or smartphones, or T-shirts. And plenty more companies that have brought a franchise to their own country or figured out a way to make a collaboration work.

The humble gumboot (or wellies as they are called in some countries) is a good example.

Years ago, an English guy called Hiram Hutchinson saw that farmers wearing wooden shoes in France kept coming home with their feet wet and muddy. When he would talk to them in the pub at night, they would complain about how much they hated their shoes. Hiram saw a problem and had a clear "*how can we*" question: *How can we* create an affordable shoe that is more comfortable and water-resistant for these French farmers?

After some research, he decided to copy a boot design that the Duke of Wellington had made for war (hence the name "wellies" now). The duke's boots went up to the knee and were made from leather, meaning that they were so expensive that only the richest British soldiers could afford them. Hiram liked the idea, but he needed to make this design more waterproof and affordable.

After some more research, he heard about a man called Charles Goodyear who had just invented the process to make rubber. After a few letters back and forth, they were able to create rubber gumboots.

Pretty simple, right?

Problem: Farmers are getting their feet wet.

Solution: Copy an old boot design but use this Goodyear's great invention called rubber to make the boots waterproof and cheap.

Result: Happy farmers and a very rich Hiram Hutchinson.

For your "*how can we*" question, take a look around the world at businesses with a product or a service that could potentially be a great answer for you, and then do one of two things:

- Reach out to them and see if they want to collaborate.

- Draw inspiration from what they and other similar companies are doing to create your own adapted idea.

To illustrate further with real-life examples, here are some ideas that we could copy, or some people we could collaborate with, to answer our question of *how can we* provide examples of affordable, high-quality schools in our country?

31. We could invite the KIPP charter schools from the United States into our country.

32. We could invite the SUCCESS charter schools from United States into our country.

33. We could invite Bridge Academies from Kenya into our country.

34. We could invite African School for Excellence from South Africa into our country.

35. We could invite High Tech High from the United States into our country.

36. We could partner with the Finnish organization HundrED to profile schools in our country.

37. We could read books about the most effective charter schools in America and try to use some of their ideas.

38. We could run a big education event similar to the BETT conference in London, or we could ask them if they want to launch a BETT conference in our country.

39. We could do a version of Khan Academy that is better suited

to our country.

40. We could reach out to Go1, the technology unicorn that acquired one of the companies that I started to see if they want to launch an online teaching academy.

Radical collaborations

Still not at 50 yet are we ...

Here is another innovation technique to get you there called "radical collaborations."

To get you warmed up, we want you to think of two random items in your house that you don't really use anymore. For example, a bicycle and a solar powered torch, or an old mobile phone and a cooking pot.

Got your two items?

Now combine the two of them to create a new product.

For example, with our mobile phone and cooking pot, we might invent a smart pot that sends a message out to everyone to come inside for dinner when the meal is ready. Or we could attach the solar torch to our bike so that we have a night light and can cycle home safely in the evening.

There are plenty of interesting real world examples out there.

The amazing Cirque de Soleil circus company and the sports

company Reebok once collaborated on a line of exercise routines, clothes, and shoes to inspire women to try some new approaches to get fit. The Sant Joan de Déu hospital in Spain collaborated with the school stationery manufacturer Miquel Rius to develop a backpack that would be kind on the spines of children even when carrying heavy loads. Blue Band margarine, sold in many countries, is fortified with vitamins A and D to be more nutritious, and a similar approach is taken by salt companies enriching their product with iodine (many people would be iodine deficient if this didn't happen). A product called Aidpods delivers vaccines and life-saving medicine in between bottles of Coca-Cola stacked in crates, using another company's logistics to deliver their product to all corners of the world.

What radical collaborations could you think up?

If we return to our question of *how can we* provide examples of affordable, high-quality schools in our country, we might consider the following:

41. Let's inspire the Pope to say that every Catholic church in the world has to have an affordable school attached to it.

42. Yes, and let's inspire the Grand Imams to say that every mosque in the world has to have an affordable school attached to it!

43. Let's launch 12 radio stations, one for each school year group, which covers the entire curriculum for five hours every day.

44. Let's inspire the local newspaper to run a two-page lesson each day, reaching a wide audience in the community.

45. Let's say that every government worker has to spend one year in every five working in a school (including the President!).

Only a few more to go to hit 50!

Set constraints

And now for one last tip to give us a final push.

Often, when we are trying to innovate solutions to a problem, it can all feel far too broad, and we can struggle to find a place to start.

A way around this is to be more specific and set some constraints on the problem.

An example could be "what if we only did our work on weekends." How would this change the responses to our question of *how can we* provide examples of affordable, high-quality schools in our country?

46. What if we ran our schools on Saturday and Sunday out of regular school buildings when they are empty, and asked for very cheap rent?

47. Yes, and what if we invited other teachers to observe our teachers in action on the weekends, to help develop their own teaching?

48. Yes, and we could get students to run a community market on Sundays to teach them entrepreneurship.

49. The school could be entirely practical, where the students start small businesses that make money on the weekends.

50. We run a school in a movie theatre for two hours in the morning, and then they get to watch a free movie on the big screen.

There we have it. We got to 50. Phew!

Picking your best idea

Having 50 ideas is great, but what we need to do now is figure out which of these are actually worth pursuing. Ultimately, you are determining here what your business model may be (well, at least which one you will test first), so it's starting to get serious, and you have some big decisions to make!

At this stage, there are two traps that people fall into.

Trap 1 is people going back to their first idea, which was always their favorite! Be careful of this, as you could really have some great ideas in the other 49 if you can just get past your love for the first one!

Trap 2 is to get excited about one idea in particular; so excited that you can't even imagine touching any of the others.

Rather than falling into either of them, stay open-minded here and consider using some of these tips to help you make an informed decision.

Tip 1 is to focus on the ideas that have the most potential to help solve the problem you have identified. With our list of 50, for example, if we are to believe the research, it's clear that one of the best ways to make a difference for kids is to ensure that their teachers are brilliant. We will probably begin by circling ideas that include this approach.

Tip 2 is to pick ideas that may be scalable (meaning they can make a big difference to a lot of people and can be repeated over and over again). Again, with our list of ideas, maybe we want to shy away from just launching one school, and instead focus on teacher training, with the idea being that if you train one great teacher, they can impact hundreds or even thousands of children.

Tip 3 is to have a good look around your country or market and determine if other people have already launched the idea you are thinking about. If they have, and they are doing it well, then you may not want to launch as a competitor. But if they are not doing a great job, or you've not seen anything like your idea in your country, power ahead! So again, for our idea, we might learn that teacher training colleges in our country do exist, are government-run, and are not highly effective. We may also find that there are plenty of great teacher training programs in other parts of the world, but in our country, we are going without.

If you were to apply these tips (high-potential ideas that are scalable and haven't been launched by someone else yet), which of your 50 would start to stick out? Which of them feel best suited to you?

You can also bring together a few ideas here. For example, if we had decided to focus on the angle of training up brilliant teachers from the countries we wanted to work in, we could highlight the following of our 50:

14. Yes, and we could also encourage great teachers from around the world to come and volunteer their services for free to keep the costs low.

29. We could start a travel company that specializes in providing field trips for excellent teachers from around the world to spend a term at schools in our country and have a great experience.

46. What if we ran our schools on Saturday and Sunday out of regular school buildings when they are empty, and asked for very cheap rent?

7. We could train up parents and grandparents to be teachers and home school their students.

OK, so this is looking interesting. A sort of local teacher training program supported by teachers who come from around the world as instructors.

It's time for you to select your one favorite idea or mash up a bunch of your best ones. Write it down here or leave a comment if you are reading along digitally.

Now give it a name

As compelling as "a sort of digital teacher training program" may be, we can probably do better. We will start with Awesome Academy. It's not a great name, but it's a start and it breathes some life into the concept.

What is the name of your best idea? Don't overthink it, it's just a working title. Once you have something, be sure to write it down.

Prototyping

At this point, things can feel really exciting.

With our Awesome Academy idea, for example, we are already feeling like it could really make a difference, people are going to love it, and lives will be changed.

Or ... it could suck.

One of the fastest ways to gain insight into whether your selected idea is going to be awesome or whether it is going to suck is to prototype it.

The word prototype is derived from the Greek word *prōtos*, which means "earliest" or "first." It is, as it sounds, the first attempt at an idea.

Prototyping gets a concept out of our head and into the world so we can start to get feedback from people who have opinions worth listening to.

Different industries prototype in different ways. For example, when car manufacturers are working on a new model, they will make a life-size version of it out of clay. They can then invite other designers, potential customers, or advisers to give them feedback on the shape they have come up with. If someone (who is worth listening to!) says "maybe this part over the front tires could be a little lower," the designers can literally just shave off some clay and then say, "How about now, is that better?"

Fashion designers also prototype. When they do a big fashion show and send out a group of models to strut down the catwalk in their new designs, they are expecting to sell only some of the items to stores, rather than everything. They want to quickly learn what people like. This freedom of knowing that not everyone is going to love every item allows them to trial ideas, push boundaries, and experiment with where they think the market may be headed.

When you are prototyping your idea, there are plenty of approaches you can consider beyond clay and catwalks. Let's explore two.

CHAPTER 5

Storyboarding

When the cartoonists and storytellers at Disney come up with their next big movie, they storyboard the idea using basic sketches on paper. Once they have a rough idea down, they can quickly ask for feedback from other members in the team.

At this early stage, things are kept very basic, and no-one is being assessed on their drawing skills. Instead, they are trying to present the idea quickly and get some insights into how it can be better.

Storyboards are a particularly good technique to represent a process or service approach like we are suggesting with our example Awesome Academy. With a storyboard at its most simple, all you do is divide a piece of paper into six or more squares and then sketch the story of what happens with your business idea. You can see an example of how we have done this below, using pretty basic little sketches and just trying to express the idea simply. (Try to use sketches rather than writing; it is easier for people to envisage in the real world this way.)

Here's a basic storyboard for Awesome Academy.

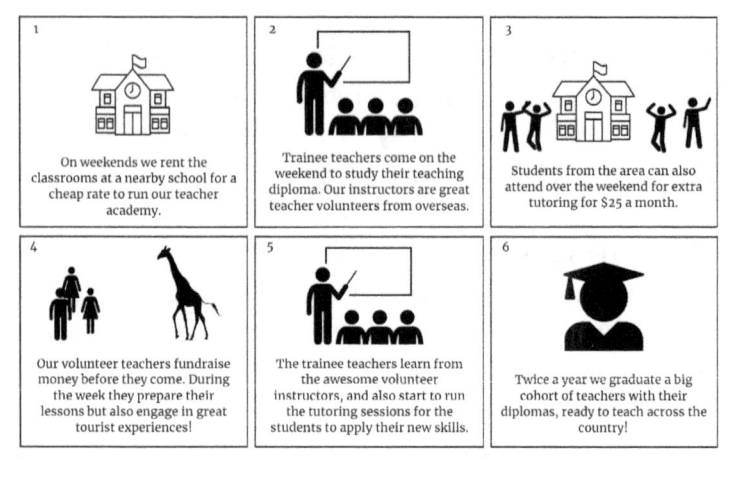

After we sketch this storyboard for Awesome Academy we want to show it to some people. Maybe we could consider:

- Some teachers friends we know in San Francisco and Ghana who may be interested in becoming one of our "awesome volunteer teachers."

- Some trainee teachers at a nearby teacher training college (but we would need to be careful to avoid the teacher training college getting upset that we are trying to poach their customers!).

- The parents of some children in the community where we are thinking we might set up to see if they would pay for their children to attend the weekend classes.

- Someone in the government of the region or country where we want to launch to see if we may be able to get funding for the teacher training we are doing.

If we were to speculate, perhaps our teacher friends from Ghana and San Francisco said the longest they could volunteer would be a month at a time. Maybe the trainee teachers told us that they wanted the diploma to be accredited by a university in Europe or the United States as they thought this would look good on their resume. Perhaps the government official was excited by the idea, but also stressed that the teachers would have to be accredited in certain areas specific to the rules of their country. Or the parents were interested in attending the weekend classes with their children to learn some things themselves, opening up some adult learning possibilities. This is all really interesting feedback for us (even though we may not integrate all of it).

With one quick storyboard on a piece of paper, we are already getting some really good insights into our Awesome Academy idea.

Let's take a look at the second way we could do a prototype.

Persona prototype

This is creating a fictional customer, detailing a challenge they have, and then proposing our solution to them.

For our Awesome Academy example, we could create a few personas, but perhaps we choose to focus on the teachers who may be learning at our academy. We've called our persona Eager Eve.

Persona Prototype: Eager Eve

The Situation

Eve is Kenyan. She did well in high school and has always wanted to be a teacher. She is very innovative and often thinks about launching her own school one day to provide an education that is more engaging and creative than what she experienced as a student. She has heard about teacher training college, but the fees are quite high, and a friend of hers said that the course was not practical and boring at times. She would love to study abroad but cannot save the money for this.

The Solution

Eve hears about Awesome Academy and decides to come by for a visit. After her tour she is so excited that she decides to sign up for the next cohort. She is able to afford the tuition costs, which are $1,200 for her to receive her basic teaching diploma. She organises for much of this cost to be repaid on a student loan. While she is in Awesome Academy, she learns through a blend of in-person lessons, practical placements with students on weekends, and video lessons that she does on her loaned tablet device each evening. After a 20 week course she is able to find work as a teacher, and hopes to return for her advanced course in a few years.

Once we have written this prototype (complete with a bad stick drawing), we could run it by some recent high-school graduates to see if they know someone like Eve. If we can find a person similar to her, we could get her feedback and then consider using it to adjust our idea.

For example, we may find out that she thinks borrowing US$1,200 as a student loan to complete the course is too expensive.

Or she may say that she would prefer a shorter, more intensive course rather than the full 20 weeks.

This is all great feedback that helps us improve our offering, and we are one step closer to making it a reality.

More ways to prototype

Remember when you are prototyping an idea, you are simply trying to help people understand what you are doing, and then asking for their honest feedback. This means that there are plenty of other ways that you can source quick, low-risk, and free insights.

Sometimes, for example, when we are launching a phone app, we do some basic mock-ups of how it may work, either on a slide-deck, using a basic app builder online, or even just sketching it on some paper.

Similarly, if your idea is to create a website, you can do a basic landing page to demonstrate to potential customers what it will look like and how they can engage with it. Again, this can be done as a sketch, as a basic document on your computer, or with a quick mock-up with the many website builders online that will let you do this for free.

If it is a physical product, you can make a very basic model to bring it into the real world, and ask people if they like the size, the color, and how it might look once it is built. This can be made with cardboard, paper, some sticky tape, and a marker pen. Or some companies will also create samples for a small cost which you can show to your potential customers.

If we are running a workshop or a hackathon with entrepreneurs, we often have a bag of Lego bricks with us to allow people to build quick prototypes of their ideas. The great thing about this technique is that you can move things around quickly based on the feedback you receive.

Again, the best thing to do now is to stop reading and spend some time building your prototype and then reaching out to some friends, family members, or potential customers to get some feedback. Remember to receive all feedback with an open mind, because as much as it may hurt, it is much better to get honest opinions now rather than a year after you have launched the business when you find yourself running out of money!

Now you've got some good ideas, it's time to test them.

CHAPTER 5

1. It is unacceptable that ✓
2. We believe ✓
3. But right now the reality is that ✓
4. The root cause we are going to focus on is ✓
5. The ideas ✓

Chapter 6

CHAPTER 6

Test the best

As we discussed in the last chapter, prototyping is great because it helps us get feedback quickly and cheaply, all while taking very little time and with minimal financial risks.

The testing phase is where we are really going to see how good our idea is, because we are going to involve real customers. Most importantly, we are moving beyond just friendly and honest feedback to see if they are willing to actually buy what we are selling.

We'll explain how a test works with a profit enterprise sock company we once started.

We had the idea to sell all our socks during the month of October, so naturally we called it Socktober.

Our plan was to sell as many pairs of bright, crazy socks as we could in that single month, encouraging people to fill up their sock drawers for the next year, and buy gifts for the holidays if they celebrated them. All the profits would go to supporting startup impact entrepreneurs across the world.

Prototyping this was easy. We:

- showed people a page with five different designs and asked them to pick their favorites; and

- had some actual sock samples made up for US$10 each design and asked people if they would buy something like this;

After a week of gaining feedback from people who shared our co-working space, we felt like we had enough positive reactions and were confident enough to move ahead.

But before we ordered 5,000 pairs of socks from the factory, we had to test if people REALLY wanted to buy our socks, or if they were just being polite when they told us how much they loved them.

So we decided on three designs, and went back to all the people we had talked to. They had all been so friendly at the prototype stage, so we were feeling upbeat. We showed them our amazing design samples, let them feel how soft the organic cotton was, talked about how the socks were made (locally with good prices going to the makers), and then told them the price (US$15 a pair).

Then we got out our order form and asked them how many they wanted to buy.

It didn't go well.

Of the 50 people who had been so positive and polite to us before, only five of them agreed to buy. This meant we only had a 10% conversion rate from the 50 warm leads we thought we had during our prototype stage.

When it comes to user experience, the saying goes, "Customers are never wrong, but they are always fascinating." So rather than get angry, we did our best to stay "fascinated" by what our customers were doing and saying.

We were told by some that they bought their socks cheap, once a year, from a discount store. They didn't seem to think quality or socially- and environmentally-conscious supply lines were important.

Others said that they were not extroverted or confident enough to wear bright, crazy socks, but they may be open to buying some plain colors (like black, black, or, at a stretch, black).

A few more told us that they would buy the socks at US$10 per pair, and someone even suggested that they'd be excited by US$50 for seven pairs (which we could sell as a "weekly pack").

We had some thinking to do.

Our profit margin would obviously be smaller with the socks at US$10, but if we sold a greater quantity would we make more money?

Did we want to spend our days selling boring black socks?

We landed on a couple of product tweaks.

- We brought the price down to US$10.
    - We created a "weekly" pack (with six black pairs of and one crazy design to help people live it up once a week).

We then went back to our 50 friends from our prototype phase and got our order form out again. We kicked our conversion rate from only five people to 17. Win.

But we still weren't convinced that we were going to launch a sock company and order 5,000 pairs just yet.

We decided we needed to run a few more tests.

CHAPTER 6

The markets

Many a product entrepreneur has made their start at local markets, setting up early in the morning with a trestle table, a few boxes worth of stock, and an open mind.

As customers peruse the stalls, the idea is to offer samples (only if that works, we couldn't offer part of a sock), get creative with your sales taglines to see what makes people stop at your stall, and see if and what they buy from you. Local markets are particularly good for food or drink products.

With our socks, we put in a small order of 100, even though we knew we had to absorb a higher unit price ordering so few. On our first market day, we were among the earliest to arrive. We ordered a coffee, laid out our socks on the table, and then started the day at the initial US$15 price point (the market often brought in well-off tourists, and we were curious if they would buy at the higher price). Our apartment was close to the market, so one of us was able to run home whenever we came up with a new idea that we needed something for. As we moved through the day, we made some tweaks:

- We quickly moved the price point back down to US$10.

- Kaitlin ran home and grabbed a plate of cookies she had baked the night before, and we started offering "free cookies." This brought people over to our table, where we would try to steer the conversation towards our great socks. In fact, these cookies were such a hit we considered pivoting our entire business to cookies!

- I ran home to get a speaker so we could play music. While I was away, Kaitlin sold seven pairs of socks, so clearly she was better at sales!

- We started the day leading with the social mission, with signs and telling people "you can help the world just by buying these great socks!" We found, though, after a few experiments, that people were far more open to the message "Christmas gifts for Dad sorted!" This brought them over, and then the social mission was an extra cherry for them.

- By the end of the first day, it was very clear which sock designs we would be running with and which we wouldn't (all the unloved designs were what we would wear ourselves for the next three years). We started to remove the unpopular versions and hide them under the table.

All in all, it helped us to drop the unpopular designs, lead with a "gifting" marketing tagline rather than social justice, and drop our price point. The music and cookies weren't scalable, so we didn't move ahead with them!

Crowdfunding

Crowdfunding is another great way to test your product.

For the uninitiated, crowdfunding can be done on sites like Kickstarter and Indiegogo.

Here is how it works:

- You put your product up for sale, clearly sharing what it does and why it is so great. Usually, you post a video, with some wording attached.

- People select from a bunch of pricing options, e.g., one at US$5, one at US$25, one at US$100, etc.

- If you make enough sales to hit the tipping point (which you set, let's say US$25,000), then people get charged for their products and you need to make them and send them.

We have seen that when this is done well, it can be really powerful.

One company, called Enda (disclaimer: we are investors in Enda), has completed two successful crowdfunding campaigns for their Kenyan-designed running shoes. Both netted them hundreds of thousands of dollars in sales.

Some tips that one of their co-founders, Navalayo, shared about running a crowdfunding campaign are:

- Traffic: You want to get as much traffic as possible to your crowdfunding page. This traffic will come through your own email list, media buzz you can create, and, if you are really lucky, being selected by your platform (e.g., Kickstarter) as a product they love. Enda was able to build their email list by appealing to runners and offering discounts to people who gave their details through the site. With the media, they made a big deal about the novelty of Kenyan-designed shoes, and in particular highlighting how it was the first time that the country famous for such successful marathon runners was now creating its own shoes! This saw them being profiled on the BBC and in runners' magazines. While they had great exposure, Nava often points out that it is maybe better to think of these campaigns as peer-funding, because the initial push of sales is likely to come from people who are already in your peer network.

- Conversion: You want to convert as many people as possible who get to your page. Having real and clear insights into the product is important here, and make sure you are nimble and can respond quickly as needed if people are asking questions. For example, Enda found that people were unsure of sizing, so quickly added expanded sizing charts and relevant information to the crowdfunding page.

- Price point: Interestingly, US$25 is the most commonly supported amount on crowdfunding campaigns. This can be tricky if your product is more expensive than that (e.g., the Enda shoe is US$100), so you want to be pushing your buyers to spend more by offering great value and additions for the higher-priced offerings. Or you can offer up a smaller product (e.g., a running T-shirt or socks) so people can engage at the lower price point. Also note that your price point may be different in your market.

Beyond these tips, there are a bunch of other things to consider when you try to test your idea with a crowdfunding campaign.

- What will get people's attention? Is there a publicity stunt that you can consider to make some noise?

For example, Simon Griffiths, a friend of ours and a former board member at an organization we started, launched a toilet paper company with some co-founders called Who Gives a Crap. They kicked off with a crowdfunding campaign that saw him sitting on a toilet until he raised US$50,000 of pre-orders. They live streamed the stunt, it took 58 hours, and they were able to get a huge buzz going about the new idea. Importantly, this stunt was directly linked to their product and was interesting enough to be shared rapidly by people.

Be careful before you commit to something like this, however, and make sure you've got a big PR and media push behind it. We've seen some stunts not go as well, such as a very wealthy entrepreneur who decided to sleep in his tent in the backyard of his mansion until he raised a set amount of money for his charity. People didn't connect with the idea, and, after a few nights, with very little money coming in, he packed up his tent and quietly came back inside. But hey, we love the commitment, and not every idea works!

- Think about the timing: Trends for 30-day crowdfunding campaigns show that around a quarter of your supporters will back you in the first few days; the next quarter or so will trickle in over the life of the campaign; and, rather scarily, the final half will come in as a final, urgent push as the deadline looms. This means you need to ensure that as many of your friends, family, and contacts from your email list are going to buy as soon as you launch. This gives some momentum and shows to others that this is a legitimate campaign that will most likely reach its target. Then, during the campaign, you want to be making as much noise as possible to help that next quarter trickle in, and by the time the last week of the campaign rolls around, enough people have seen it enough times that you can finally convince them to commit.

How else can you test it?

Remember, at this stage of your business, all you are trying to do is see if people want to buy what you are selling. Maybe you could give some free product to a social media influencer to see if they like it, and gauge their openness to being a brand ambassador?

You could run a Google Ads campaign to determine what you'd need to spend on marketing your product to get people to your website.

You could try getting some predictive answers from Google, where you type in the first word or two of your product and see what people are often searching for with similar products. For example, you might type in "running shoes" and the predictive text might say:
   Running shoes are too expensive.
   Running shoes that don't hurt my feet.
   Running shoes that I can wear to work.

This gives you some insights into what problems people have, and you can consider tailoring your product to solve them. As the saying goes, try to be a painkiller for people (by solving their issue) rather than a multivitamin (a weak promise for a possible long-term improvement in their life).

Could you gift some product to your friends and family and then have them come over to dinner and give you really honest feedback?

Could you try the product thoroughly yourself? For example, with Enda shoes, their founders wore them every day in all sorts of environments to see how comfortable and durable they were (and to see how many comments they received).

Could you try to sell your product on consignment, where you give it to a local store, get it on their shelf and give them a commission for what they sell? Keep testing your idea, and keep improving it based on the feedback you are getting.

The bad boyfriend concept

Something to keep in mind at this stage of your idea is what is often referred to as the "bad boyfriend concept."

This is where you have a boyfriend (or girlfriend) who never buys you a birthday or Valentine's Day present. They never take you on dates, they are always late, they are rarely nice to you, and you occasionally hear rumors that they are maybe not being faithful to you. Ever dated someone like this?

Sometimes, we can fall into the trap of thinking that if we just love this person a bit more, are nicer to them, and shower them with presents and dates that with time they will turn things around and become an amazing partner.

Now, the reality (which all your family and friends want to tell you!) is that you simply have a bad boyfriend on your hands, and it's time to break up with them.

Now, imagine your current idea is the boyfriend.

There's no doubt you are excited about it.

But let's say you tested it with a bunch of your friends and only a few of them bought it.

Or the results of the market tests you ran weren't great.

Or the crowdfunding campaign is a bit of a flop.

On the one side, you could be lured into thinking, *If I just put some more money into Facebook ads* or, *My friends aren't very stylish and they wouldn't appreciate this product*, or, *Maybe it just needs more time, so I will extend the end date on the crowdfunding campaign.*

Or … you could realize you maybe have a bad boyfriend on your hands, and know that it's time to break up with the idea.

How to kill off an idea

If you've realized you need to kill off the idea, just do it. It should be easy.

Here are a few reasons why.

- You almost definitely don't have any employees that you have to let go, which is one of the hardest parts of closing down a company (if you have already hired staff while testing, you probably shouldn't have!). Given it is more than likely just you working on it at this stage, have a short moment of sadness, then smile and get back to work inventing the idea that will actually work!

- You probably don't have a large amount of physical stock purchased and sitting in a warehouse during the testing phase (again, if you have, that is a mistake), so there is very little to sell off or throw away.

- No-one will care. This is tough to hear, we know, but the reality is that very few people are going to care that this business idea wasn't a good one. Obviously, you care, and your mother might also care, but you don't need to worry about anyone else's feelings. In fact, the chances are if you never bring it up again in conversation, no-one else will either.

If it's time to kill off the bad idea, simply send out an email, if you feel it's necessary, to let people know what is happening (which they may not read), and then get back to finding the idea that will work. The only people you probably need to contact are the people you bought your samples from, or the web designer who might have helped you with your basic site, or the few die-hard customers who fell in love with your idea. Of course, if you did the full crowd-funding campaign and reached your financial goal, it's going to be more complex as you'll need to execute on that campaign and send people all their products.

Killing off an idea like this might feel like a failure, but never forget that this the good kind of failure, and you shouldn't feel sad about it.

Instead, be happy that you tested small and that you can pivot easily. Imagine if you had wasted the next three years of your life on this bad idea! The silver lining is that you are now one step closer to finding the one thing that will work. As Thomas Edison, who famously got the lightbulb idea wrong 10,000 times before he finally cracked it, once said: "I failed my way to success."

And, remember, you have 49 other ideas sitting on that list you made, and you are probably still passionate about helping to solve that root cause you circled.

How to move forward with an idea

It's not all doom and gloom. Maybe your test went well, and you want to go ahead with it. Which is great! You are ready to move to the next step.

What you need to keep in mind, though, is that this idea is far from fully baked yet, so it's still premature to go out and raise capital and grow rapidly.

At this stage, it is very much just a prototype that has survived some basic testing.

In fact, it is probably so basic that you are going to laugh at it one day when you look back at its current state.

But saying this, it's time to get moving. In fact, if you aren't slightly embarrassed by your first offering you've probably taken too long to get to market.

This means you should take all that feedback you've received, bring some of it onboard to improve your product, put some of it aside (not all of it is useful, and you will never please everyone), take a quick breath, and then get ready for the next stage of your journey as an impact entrepreneur.

1. It is unacceptable that ✓
2. We believe ✓
3. But right now the reality is that ✓
4. The root cause we are going to focus on is ✓
5. The ideas ✓
6. Test the best ✓

Chapter 7

Does it solve the problem in a scalable and sustainable way?

Excellent. Your idea passed the various tests of Step 6.

This means that a few people purchased your product or service, liked it, and then a few more did.

CHAPTER 7

You feel confident that there is a business concept here that is worth pursuing.

Time to go big, right?

Well, almost ...

Before you start to build your pitch deck to raise millions of dollars, take out a lease on a new company headquarters, hire a founding team, and start reaching out to *Fast Company* magazine to be on their front cover, we've still got some foundational work to do.

The good news is that a lot of step 7 can be done at home, working through some numbers and hypotheticals to see if things make business sense.

Which means it's time to get a calculator, some paper, and a pen ready and step through this next little bit carefully with us.

If you are reading the short introduction to this step thinking, *This finance stuff is not really for me*, you more than anyone need to make sure you read this carefully! Don't worry, we will keep it simple; and believe us when we say that with these basics, you will start to feel like finance isn't all that bad!

Let's start by looking over the various components of your business model.

A profit or process enterprise?

Remember back a few steps to where we were helping you come up with 50 ideas, we talked about the difference between profit and process impact businesses?

As we discussed, a profit impact business is a very simple structure. Here the goal is to make a profit (usually the case in a business), with the idea that those profits, or a percentage of those profits, will be directed to an impact mission. The impact side of the equation is therefore likely making a loss financially, but it is paid for by the profit-making side.

If you are going down the route of a profit impact business, you have one very big question to ask yourself, which is: *Will I make enough profit to direct a meaningful amount of money to a cause?*

Some people fall into the trap of thinking that if a business is making money then surely there will be some to give away. But this is certainly not always the case. To put this in perspective, the average restaurant has a profit margin of 5%, meaning there is rarely a large pot of money sitting around at the end of each month or each financial year. Just think of all that activity in a restaurant – food being ordered from suppliers, diners being fed, dishes being washed, staff being paid – and at the end of a good week there may only be a 5% profit. Based on these margins, it can be very hard to make a restaurant a meaningful profit impact business. (We learned this the hard way, so trust us on this one.)

The other type we mentioned earlier is the process impact

business. This is where the actual day to day running of the company is creating the impact. And interestingly, after we've just questioned the wisdom of starting a restaurant, with this structure it might work better. For example, Streat is a network of cafés in Melbourne, Australia. Their business model is simple. They train and hire at-risk young people to work in their cafés. Therefore, the more coffees, sandwiches, and cakes they sell, the more jobs they create, and the more people they can help.

Sama is another process impact business. It is a technology organization that secures contracts from major companies across the globe and hires technology workers in emerging markets to deliver on those jobs. The last time we looked they had secured a bunch of big AI training jobs with some huge firms in the US, adding to the many lives they have already impacted across Africa and Asia.

A big question you need to ask with a process impact business (well, any business, to be honest) is:

Will we be able to make enough money to keep running the business in the way that we want to?

Imagine, in the early days of their business a company like Sama secures a technology contract for US$220,000 from Microsoft (let's say it's an AI program that can identify images). But if it costs them US$400,000 to cover the office, training program, wages, and management team to deliver on this contract, then this business model is not working for them. Quite simply, they lost US$180,000 in this deal. They may be able to prop this up with grants and donations, but if this were the case, they would be leaning away from being a business and more of a non-profit (nothing wrong with that, it's just important to note!). Equally, they may also be willing to take investment money in the early years and work at a loss to build up their processes and their brand. But at some point, they need to feel like they have a model that could be profitable or at least cover costs.

Another question you will need to ask in a process impact business is: What will we have to compromise to make the business financially sustainable?

If you remember earlier in the book, we talked about the group in South Africa who train and employ men who have found themselves in challenging situations. They are a process impact business, and their idea is to make furniture and sell it locally. If they were just a regular furniture company, they could copy some fashionable designs that they've seen in magazines, have some pieces manufactured in China, and sell them through eBay at the lowest possible price. Importantly, though, the purpose of their work is not to just sell furniture, but instead to change the lives of the men they support. This means that they must spend time teaching these men how to make furniture. They face the risk of having a less consistent product than one a Chinese factory can produce at scale. Their cost may be higher per piece of furniture. And the chances are with this process business model, they won't be a serious competitor to Ikea. But they don't want to be. They are willing to compromise on a range of things to maximize their social mission.

Weighing up the two business approaches (profit and process), it's important to ask yourself which approach would make the bigger impact.

Let's stick with Hands of Honor as our example.

If we went for the profit-style company, maybe we could launch an affordable furniture company, get our furniture made in China, and sell it locally in South Africa. Maybe in a good first year we could do US$100,000 of sales, with a profit margin of 10% (meaning we have made a profit of US$10,000). Maybe we could give away some of our furniture stock to homes looking after at-risk men. Or maybe we would want to donate our US$10,000 of profit to community projects. We would also need to consider keeping some of that US$10,000 to pay for staff if times are tough in the months ahead or prepare for the next shipment of furniture. Maybe we should also consider keeping some of this profit to invest in the company website to try to sell more furniture in the future. These are all tough decisions.

Using the process business approach, perhaps we could train and employ seven men that year and do US$40,000 of sales with very little to no profit margin.

Which is better, in your opinion? There is no right answer here, by the way. To be honest, it comes down to which business model you think you can make work; and, importantly, the approach that you are inspired to make work as well. But understanding the financial realities of both the profit and process approach is important.

Now returning to your idea, which approach makes the most sense? Profit or process? Do the basic numbers work?

To quickly recap:

- You've been inspired to solve a problem.

- You've spent some time trying to understand it better.

- You've innovated a load of ideas, tested a few, and moved ahead with one of them.

- You've figured out if it is a profit or process enterprise.

Some basic finances.

Very basic, in fact; don't worry, this is not going to turn into an accounting book. We just want to give you an initial understanding of a few essential numbers for your business.

Over time, you will need to learn more, of course, and there are a few ways you can do this:

- You can partner up with someone who has a good brain for finances, either as a co-founder or, if you can afford it or convince someone to do it very cheaply, have a finance expert on your team, even if it is just half a day a week to begin with.

- You can try to learn it yourself. If you take this route, there's no need to go crazy and do a three-year accounting degree. Instead, there are some great resources you can draw on quickly, with one of our favorites being the book *Street Smarts* by Bo Burlingham and Norm Brodsky.

Or you already know finances well and don't need any of this!

But for us less financially minded, let's get into the basics.

There is a common tendency at this early stage of your business to think, *OK, I can get this thing made for this much, sell it at this much, and that leaves this much profit every time I make a sale. This is going to be a huge success!*

As you progress, however, you will quickly see that things are more complicated. Rather than being surprised by this complexity, it can be wise to do some groundwork now to try to better understand what it is costing you to get your product or service to a customer.

The fancy term for this analysis is "unit economics," but basically it calculates how much it is ACTUALLY costing you to sell.

We will run through this quickly here to give you a better idea of your situation. It's worth noting that your unit economics will change with time. Usually, in the early days of a business, you are hustling to get things for free, or you are working out of your house just to get things up. So, as you get more serious your costs may grow. But equally, as you grow, you can sometimes access "economies of scale" where you can buy in bulk at lower prices and improve the efficiency of your processes and production. So this first swing at unit economics is just that, a first swing to roughly see if the business makes sense.

Your first step is to identify what your unit is. When people are asked this question, their initial response is to think of their unit as their product, but this is not correct. Instead, your unit is the *person* who pays for the product.

We will use a shoe company as an example to help identify our unit.

Our basic idea is to sell basketball shoes, and then we want to use the profits we make to support basketball programs for at-risk youths in Chicago. We may sell our shoes through our own online store. If that is the case, our unit is the person who is buying our shoes through the website. This approach would make you a B2C (business to consumer) company.

Alternatively, rather than selling through our website, we could sell our shoes directly to other fashion outlets (both online and through retail stores). In this case, the unit is those shoe shops. This makes us a B2B (business to business) company.

Take a moment now to think about your unit, and whether you are a B2C or B2B company. Remember, B2C is where you sell directly to customers and B2B is where you sell wholesale to other businesses.

If you are thinking, *Hang on, I plan to do both*, that's OK. It just means your business modeling is going to be a little more complex.

CHAPTER 7

The second step is to then figure out what your unit costs are. This is not what you sell the unit for (another common mistake), but rather you are determining the cost of selling one unit.

Let's do this for our B2C shoe company (where we sell directly to our customers through our website). We need to determine the costs that go into making a shoe and selling it online. With an initial production run of 1,000 shoes, here are some of the costs that we have thought about:

- We are launching with one initial model of basketball shoe that we are calling the "Toro." We are having these built in a shoe factory in Turkey, and the best price we could find, for the quality we wanted, with good conditions for workers, was US$26 a pair delivered to our Chicago headquarters.

- Each designed cardboard box that contains the shoes cost US$2.20.

- We attach a label to each pair of shoes at our HQ. These cost US$0.60 each.

- We want to put a flyer with the story of our company in the box, and each flyer costs US$0.10.

- We include free shipping with our shoes, as we think we need to do this to be competitive. This costs US$8.70.

- Our marketing campaign is largely focused on social media. We are finding that for each US$100 we spend on targeted social media ads, we get 52 visits to our site. Of these hits, we then get 13 sales. So that means each sale is costing us US$7.70 in marketing.

- As the two co-founders, we are the only staff currently and are doing all the postage, social media, enquiries ... well, everything really. We are using laptops that we already own to run the company, and we have WIFI as part of our apartment lease. We are factoring in US$5 per sale for our wages to help us pay our rent.

- We offer a guarantee that if people aren't happy with the Toro shoe they can return them for free within the first week, and have had some returns in the last few months, but not too many. We factor in US$2 per pair of shoes for this.

- Friends volunteer as our accountants and lawyers, so there is no cost there just yet. Remember, though, that these free breaks are unlikely to last as you grow and become more serious.

- Unfortunately, we don't have the space in our apartment to store 1,000 pairs of shoes, but there is a YMCA that let us use a spare room for free.

- To register the business cost us close to US$1,000 in fees. So, that is US$1 a pair for the first run, but it's a one-time cost.

What else are we missing? It's hard to keep track of all the little costs that keep adding up, so we've decided to keep a record of every expense in the notes section of our smartphone for this first 1,000 pair of shoes.

At this stage, this is all very startup. Or, to use a common term, we are "bootstrapping" it. We are calling in as many favors as we can and trying to keep costs low. So far, here are our costs per pair of shoes:
- Shoe manufacture and shipping to us: US$26
- The box: US$2.20
- Label: US$0.60
- Flyer: US$0.10
- Shipping to the customer: US$8.70
- Social media: US$7.70
- Staff stipend: US$5
- Guarantee: US$2
- Accountants and lawyers: US$0
- Storage: US$0
- Registering the business: US$1

So, that is US$53.30, at the moment, to get a shoe to a customer. That's our unit cost. It's an OK number if we can keep costs this lean. And, remember, we are barely paying ourselves anything yet.

We are going to put US$20 aside per shoe to help us finance the next run (we want to order 5,000 pairs if we sell the first 1,000 Toros).

It's important to note here that some of these costs are fixed (the things that you absolutely have to spend month on month to be a shoe company), and some are variable (i.e., we are making a decision to have something extra to add value, like the flyer we put in the box or the guarantee we have for returns). Every expense we choose to bring on will raise the unit cost. Every time we make a saving, or compromise, or find a better deal for something, the unit cost goes down. Improving our unit economics means more money directed to the inner-city basketball program we want to be supporting. One thing that can quickly blow out your unit cost is when you give away items. It can be really tempting to give a pair to yourself, your friends, an influencer that you think will be able to help you sell more shoes, or someone else that you think would think you are cool if you throw them a free pair of Toros! But every time you do, your unit cost will go up. Be wary of falling into this trap, which is particularly easy to do in hospitality, where a free coffee, drink, or meal here and there adds up.

The next thing we need to think about is our customer lifetime value. Basically, we are trying to figure out how much money can we make from our customers, how many times over. If we were an insurance company, our customer lifetime value is high, because if we keep our customers, we get paid by them every month, often for years. As a shoe company, however, there is a very real chance someone buys from us only once, or perhaps every few years if we are lucky. Bummer. But there are ways to try to increase the lifetime value for our shoe customers. Enda shoes, for example, have a subscription program for their most committed runners, where they send a new pair of shoes to them every three months.

As we continue with our unit economics, we want to try to understand the customers we are targeting with the Toro basketball shoe. Here you can ask yourself a few important questions:

- Do you know who your customers are? We will dig some more into our customer base in the marketing section, but for now we are trying to get a rough sense of who might buy our products. The good news with basketball shoes is that they are not just purchased by basketball players; plenty of people buy them as fashion statements too. Do you know who your customers are likely to be?

- Do you know how many potential customers there are? We see plenty of startups getting excited about the size of their market very early in the game. For example, a soap company might say, "There are 45 million people living in the UK, and they all need to buy soap, therefore if we can just get 10% of the market, we will have 4.5 million customers a year!" At this early stage, however, we aren't all that interested in how many people in Chicago, or the United States, or the world, might want to buy basketball shoes, because those numbers become unrealistic for a startup very quickly. If our first run of shoes is 1,000 pairs, we may have some degree of confidence (based on our research and the connections we have in Chicago) that there are at least 1,000 people out there who may be interested in our shoes.

Based on the insights above about our unit, our unit costs, our customer lifetime value, and who and how many customers we may have to engage with, we've innovated a few ideas.

In the early days, to help sell our first 1,000 pairs, we are aiming to do a little bit of influencer-based marketing where we ask well-known fashion and basketball influencers in Chicago and the wider United States to spread the word about our shoes. We are hoping that the good vibes they feel about the community projects they are supporting by buying our shoes will encourage them to share our story for free. We are also going to print out some flyers and posters and put them up around basketball facilities, outside the Chicago Bulls basketball arena, and in nightclubs (which will, of course, add to our unit cost!).

To try to increase our customer lifetime value, we are focusing on how we can build customer loyalty and keep them coming back to buy more. We have decided to launch the "Hoops" club. If you buy a pair of shoes from us, you can become a member of the Hoops club, which gives you a 5% discount on Chicago Bulls tickets (we've managed to strike a social justice partnership with them) and also early access to sales. You also get a 5% discount on your future shoe orders from us (but we will also give you the chance to donate that 5% discount to our partner projects).

To try and get our customers to buy more of our shoes, we've decided to trial a new shoe release annually, in collaboration with a Chicago artist or basketballer. This will hopefully encourage people to buy a pair each year or, at the very least, bring in new customers who love these collaborators. We are hoping for Michael Jordan or Scotty Pippen next year (hey, we can always dream!).

We are also interested in the average transaction size, meaning, quite simply, when people buy from us, how much are they usually handing over. The obvious answer would be US$100, the price we've set for the Toros, but are there ways we can increase this (given all the hard work we have put in to make them a customer!)? We've thought about giving a 10% discount if you buy two pairs of shoes (marketing this as "have an everyday pair and a fancy pair!"). Or, we are looking at making a slightly cheaper shoe in smaller kids' sizes, the idea being that you would buy a pair for yourself and then a pair for US$50 as a gift for a child in your life. We've decided to keep this on the backburner for now, however, and not launch the kids' line as we can't get the unit cost low enough, but we'll consider testing it later.

Now we need to make sure we are happy with our price point.

We've decided on US$100, because we think it is comparable to other basketball shoes on the market (cheaper than Air Jordans and a whole lot cheaper than another Chicagoan Kanye West's Yeezys). This is going to include shipping across the US, but for now we can't ship internationally (it's just going to get too expensive and complex for this early stage). We don't know if people will buy our shoes at US$100, but we are crossing our fingers and toes that they will.

We have committed to avoiding discount sales or voucher codes, because we know that if we put any kind of discount on these, we will quickly compromise our unit economics and eat into the amounts we can send to our local community project.

Got all that?

So far, we have:
- Identified and got to know our unit.
- Determined our unit cost.
- Looked at our customer lifetime value.
- Thought more about our customers.
- Decided on our price point.

Now, this is just a very shallow sweep through unit economics, designed to give you an insight into the price you might charge and the costs you will incur to get your product (or service) to the customer. There are plenty of things we can tweak here, but at least we know the impact it is having. And this is the important thing with unit economics. It's that you truly understand the costs for your product and keep a close eye on them. If you don't, it's like being in a plane without a pilot (or where the pilot is in the back having a cup of tea with the stewards). You need to be up front, in the cockpit, understanding what is going on.

Seeing the blind spots in the business

All of us do not have as much business acumen as we'd like in certain areas.

For example, you might turn out to be great at sales but weak at creating new product. Or you could be a marketing genius who just can't seem to get your head around the finances. Or you could be a brilliant relationship builder who just can't deliver on your promises of getting quality product to your customers on time.

CHAPTER 7

A useful tool to help you think about your blind spots and gain a broader understanding of all elements of your company is the business model canvas. This nine-part overview of a business was created by Alexander Osterwalder in 2005, but since then it has been tweaked, refined, and adapted by different industries.

You might have heard of it, or filled one in if you've attended a startup bootcamp. If so, try not to fall into the trap of thinking, *Ah yes, I've done that before*, and then skip this section. What's important is whether you have done one for THIS business!

Key Partnerships	Key Activities	Value Proposition	Customer Relationships	Customer Segments
	Key Resources		Channels	

Cost Structures	Revenue Streams

How you fill this out for a profit or a process social enterprise will be slightly different.

Let's start with a process structure:

Key Partnerships: This box is for you to list which partnerships make it easy for you to operate. If you make a physical product, it may be the suppliers who make certain parts for you. Perhaps it is a transportation company or warehousing facility that gives you an affordable rate? Or perhaps it is a non-profit which identifies the people who might come through your program (i.e., prisoners who are leaving a rehabilitation program and are now looking for a job). Think about all the partnerships that make your work easier, or cheaper, or without whom you might be in trouble from a business perspective.

Key Activities: This box is for you to detail exactly what it is that you do. You may be surprised how many early-stage entrepreneurs can't answer this question! For example, you might be a training company that teaches adults to code websites. Or you are a branding company that is creatively marketing female-targeted products. You can see here that we are describing these businesses as a "training company" or "a branding company." It can be helpful to forget about your product for a moment here and try to determine what kind of company you have. Then, from this, expand to briefly explain exactly what you do. For example, you may say, "We are a food experience company that hires newly-arrived refugees and asylum seekers."

Key Resources: This box is for you to detail what you need to do to run the business. With all the unit economics work you've just done, this should be easy! Detail the machinery you might need (e.g., sewing machines in a fashion label), the equipment (e.g., pots and pans in a restaurant), the supplies (e.g., ingredients if you are a cookie company), the staff you need (e.g., sales floor staff if you are a retail shop), or your curriculum (if you are a training company). This box helps to ensure you are thinking about as many of the in-house components of the business as you can, remembering that every component takes both time and money to have as part of your business model.

Value Proposition: This box is for you to detail the value that you create for your customers. If you can't clearly state this, it's a good sign the business idea needs a lot more thinking and work. For example, you may be a cleaning company that "cleans people homes so they don't have to," or a rubbish removal company that "conveniently takes away people's unwanted items." Or you might be a healthcare company that "provides an affordable and high-quality healthcare option for the people of Kibera."

Customer Relationships: This box is for you to detail the kinds of relationships you have with your customers. This helps you plan how to stay engaged with your customers, particularly if you have invested a great deal of effort to attract them and deliver your product or service to them. If you are a food distribution company, you might "deliver grocery boxes weekly, with a letter to them in each box," or, if you are a dentist, you might "engage with our patients quarterly with advice and encourage them to book an annual check-up." If you are a training company, you may "see students at weekly classes and keep engaged with alumni through monthly emails." If you are a travel company, you may "post on social media twice a week with inspiring travel options and email our customers with monthly deals."

Customer Segments: This box is for you to detail who your customers are. Imagine you are a food experience company like Free to Feed, a social enterprise that employs refugees and asylum seekers. Some of your customers are the individuals or groups of friends that book cooking classes. Others hire you for corporate catering events. You also have some customers who like to buy your spices and sauces online through your website. While there may sometimes be overlaps between these people, it is important to understand the different groups, because this will determine the products and services you ship, and the way that you market.

Channels: This box is for you to detail how you attract customers. We will touch on marketing later in the book, but, for now, it's important to keep in mind how you think you will bring customers through the door, get them to your website, or have them give you a call. Let's say you are an events company that puts on concerts to support emerging artists. You might then be on social media platforms where you share videos of the artists playing over the next month. You might put up marketing posters around town and put flyers in bars and cafés. You might try to get your artists on local radio for interviews to spread the word. All these activities are designed to encourage people to buy tickets to your shows, but they all cost money (even if it is just your bus fare to get to the radio station), and they all take time.

Revenue Streams: This box is simple; it details how you make money. Or, more specifically, what are the ways that human beings or companies end up transferring bits of currency from their bank account to yours? For example, if you were a fitness network focused on helping women stay healthy, you may have monthly membership fees for your physical gyms, personalized coaching sessions for women, as well as vitamins, supplements, and clothing that you sell at the gyms and through your website.

Cost Structure: This box will again be easy to fill out if you have done your unit economics work, where you built a sense of how much it costs you to run the company. Let's say you are a student-tutoring company. You need to think about the rent on the space where you run your in-person classes, the salaries of the tutors, your marketing expenses to find new students, the electricity to run your computer, the cost to lease or buy furniture and computers, stationery costs per class, and plenty of other things (even including how much toilet paper the students will go through at your premises!). You can break this down monthly or yearly, but the important thing is to have a good initial understanding of your cost structure. Be more generous with the numbers than you'd like to be; costs always add up fast. Always remember to look at which costs are discretionary (i.e., you may be able to do without them) and only keep those which you think are an absolute necessity.

These are the boxes that make up the process social enterprise, where your product and service make the impact itself. If you are a profit social enterprise, however, there are some subtle differences to the canvas that you must consider. Let's jump into those using the template canvas below:

Now let's think about how you would use the canvas for a profit social enterprise. For consistency, we will use the basketball shoe business idea we discussed earlier.

Key Partnerships: In this box, we detail the partnerships that make it easy for us to run the commercial and impact arms of the business. For example, on the commercial side, these would be the manufacturers of the shoes and the shoeboxes. On the impact side, it would be our non-profit partner which runs the programs for at-risk young people in Chicago.

Key Activities: Again, on the commercial side, this box relates to the selling of our shoes, and, on the impact side, it relates to the programs that we offer. This raises a big question around whether we will run the social programs ourselves or whether we will give funding to a local non-profit to do this for us.

Key Resources: On the commercial side, in this box we would list product design, marketing, and sales logistics capacity at a minimum (even if that is coming from us in the early days). We've decided, as we look at this canvas, that we are going to connect to a non-profit now for the programming, so we won't need our own in-house impact professionals. The group we've selected is called Hoop Dreams and they use sport to engage kids in Chicago.

Value Proposition: On the commercial side, we hope that our basketball shoes are so great that people keep coming back for them. In this box, we would spell out the features that make our shoe so compelling. On the impact side, given our partnership with the social impact program Hoop Dreams, we need to make our annual transfer of funding compelling enough for them to associate with us, and put their very cool and established brand alongside ours.

Customer Relationships: In this box, we are thinking about how we engage with our customers and keep them happy. For example, perhaps we have a newsletter that maintains the connection and a referral program for our evangelist customers who can gain perks for sharing our products.

Channels: In this box, we are listing all the ways we get our product into our customers' hands. For example, we may sell online through our own website or affiliate websites, through shoes stores, or at local fashion markets.

Revenue Streams: This box is largely going to be dominated by our shoe company revenue, but perhaps we could also look at applying for some grants in partnership with Hoop Dreams?

Cost Structure: To run the shoe side of the business is one thing, but, in this box, we also need to determine how we are going to structure the costs on the impact side. Are we giving a certain amount of money to Hoop Dreams per pair of shoes sold? Or are we guaranteeing them a set amount, say US$10,000 a year? Or are we giving them a percentage of profits which we will know at the end of the year after we reconcile our finances?

There you have it, an explainer of a business model canvas for both profit- and process-driven social enterprises.

Your theory of change

One way to help determine whether your idea solves a problem in a scalable and sustainable way is with a theory of change, a strategic tool that is widely known by many professional non-profit workers, but less so by entrepreneurs.

You will quickly notice that we've been taking you through this structure step by step in the book, so this will be very easy for you to complete! We'd encourage you to complete your theory of change now, and use this as a strategic foundation as you move forward with your business.

We believe:

The first question you've already answered is what is the big goal you are aiming for? This can be huge (as in global), or localized, but we've found the easiest way to answer is with the sentence we had you complete earlier:

We believe in a .... where ...

As a reminder, some examples were:

- We believe in a world where all women can give birth safely.

Or ...

- We believe in a Kenya where everyone has access to electricity.

Or ...

- We believe in a Tsokoku where every child can access a quality education.

This sentence encapsulates the big goal.

Remember that you and your company won't achieve this alone, but rather you will be a part of the solution. As Bobby Kennedy said, "Few will have the greatness to bend history itself; but each of us can work to change a small portion of events, and in the total; of all those acts will be written the history of this generation."

If you are writing along in a physical book, or leaving a comment in an e-book, find your earlier notes and then complete this sentence again:

    We believe in a _____ where ...

_____

_____

_____

But right now, the reality is that:

The next step in your theory of change is where you looked at the current situation so you can be clear on the facts. It's important to have credible statistics here, and the sentence we want you to fill out is:

But right now, the reality is that _____

This builds on the "*We believe*" statements from above.

- *We believe* in a world where all women can give birth safely. *But right now, the reality is that,* according to the World Health Organization, more than 800 women die every day while trying to give birth.

Shocking statistic, and a very worthy problem to try to solve.

Or ...

- *We believe* in a Kenya where everyone has access to electricity. *But right now, the reality is that* 18 million Kenyans (of a total population of 51 million people) do not have access to electricity in their homes.

Or ...

- *We believe* in a Tsokoku where every child can access a quality education. *But right now, the reality is that* only one in every 10 children at the community's six schools are graduating and moving on to higher studies.

CHAPTER 7

So get your notes out from earlier in the book and complete the sentence:

But right now the reality is ...

_____
_____
_____

The root cause we are focusing on is:

The issues you are trying to solve are complex, and you can't go it alone. Rustle up that root cause tree from before, check the root that you circled, and finish the sentence:

There are many reasons why this problem exists, but *the root cause we are focusing on is ...*

For example, let's go deeper with our problem of women not giving birth safely.

- *We believe* in a world where all women can give birth safely. *But right now, the reality is that,* according to the World Health

Organization, more than 800 women die every day while trying to give birth. There are many reasons why this problem exists, but *the root cause we are focusing on is* the need for women to have access to basic medical supplies during non-hospital births.

Take a moment to detail the root cause you are focused on:

The root cause we are focusing on is ...
_____
_____
_____

What we do is:

These three points combined give us the big picture, an understanding of the current reality, and a key root cause to focus on. The next stage is simple: just explain what you do.

So, to continue with our example about safe birthing:

We run a maternity fashion label. For each item we sell in our online store, we donate a safe birthing kit to Save The Children.

Can you write in a sentence or two exactly what it is that you do?

What we do is ...

_____
_____
_____

Finally, you need to determine your impact goal, and if you have had some impact already, what that has been so far. We will talk more about impact later in the book, but for now we can keep it simple. For example:

So far, we have provided safe birthing kits to 6,200 women.

What is your current impact? (It's OK if that is zero, you might just be getting started.)

So far we have ...

_____
_____
_____

There you have it. A basic theory of change.

We believe ...

Right now, the reality is that ...

There are many reasons why this problem exists, but *the root cause we are focusing on is ...*

What we do is ...

So far, we have ...

These five sentences give you a strategic foundation to guide the actions of your business and keep you focused. If, for example, you are a few years in, and you don't have a compelling way to complete the sentence "*so far we have,*" this helps you question whether all your effort is having an impact. Or, if you have become distracted and you begin to realize that your "*what we do is*" sentence is no longer linked to the root cause you selected, then you may want to refocus your business. We often ask a simple question when we are innovating and adapting our business model:

Do we need to rethink our theory of change, or do we need to adopt a different business tactic?

If we've just become excited by a new product that is misaligned to our theory of change, it's likely that we will drop the new idea. But if we feel like the theory of change is off, we will sometimes make the big commitment to take a step back and rethink it, a decision we don't take lightly!

Market validation

Now, as we reach the end of this rather chunky chapter, you need to prove that your idea will work in the real world. We will use a new example to explain this - market validation.

Let's say we have a company in Ghana that sells environmentally friendly (clean) cookstoves.

We have decided to go after a bunch of different markets, selling to individual customers (B2C) and businesses (B2B). Specifically, we are pushing into the following markets:

B2C:

- Individual homeowners who want to move away from wood fires and charcoal, for either health or affordability reasons.
- Small restaurant owners who might like the efficiency and affordability of the stoves.
- Weekend campers who want our cookstove to take on their camping trips and are excited that we have a "buy one, give one" model.

B2B:

- Wholesale shops which are eager to meet customer demands for cleaner cooking options and are looking for products with a good profit margin.
- Non-profit organizations which are eager to provide safe, affordable, and healthy cooking facilities in refugee camps.

These are our customer segments, and they are helpful for us to understand how we should be marketing, where we need to offer customer service and support, and how we refine our product design.

We've obviously made a big assumption that these customers segments will see value in our cookstove. It can be useful to frame each of them with a value proposition sentence, which looks like this:

Our *(products/services)* help(s) *(customer group)* who want to *(what your business helps them achieve)* by *(the way your business delivers that value)* and *(another way you deliver value)*. Unlike *(main competitor)*, our product *(what you do differently)*.

Therefore, our value proposition sentences for our cookstove company could be:

Homeowners: *Our cookstoves help homeowners who want to reduce smoke in their home, save money on fuel, and save time collecting firewood and cooking, by providing a clean and affordable alternative. Unlike other clean cookstoves, our cookstoves are easy to install and can be paid off in monthly installments.*

Restaurants: *Our cookstoves help restaurants which want to be more efficient and environmentally friendly by providing a clean alternative that saves them money and time. We also offer great customer service and, unlike other clean cookstoves, our cookstoves are available in larger sizes (designed to cook large quantities) and last up to 10 years.*

Wholesale shops: *Our cookstoves help wholesale shops which want to meet their customer demands for cleaner cooking options while getting good returns, by providing a clean and affordable alternative with attractive profit margins. Unlike other clean cookstoves, our cookstoves are priced attractively and have great customer reviews.*

Non-Profit Organizations: *Our cookstoves help non-profits which want to set up affordable, safe, and clean cooking facilities in refugee camps. Unlike other clean cookstoves, our cookstoves can come in large sizes (designed to cook large quantities for larger numbers of people) and are easy to maintain.*

Weekend Campers: *Our cookstoves help weekend campers who want a clean cooking stove to take on their camping trips by providing a portable option that is light and efficient. Unlike other cookstoves, we have a compelling social mission, as when campers buy one of our stoves, we give another stove to a family in need.*

Now, with all of these ideas, we of course need to go and test them in the market.

We could start this, very simply and cheaply, by having some conversations.

For example, we could reach out to 10 non-profit organizations which are operating in refugee camps or 100 weekend campers to gauge their interest.

In our experience, though, and as we discussed with our sock experiment, while conversations have some use, they are not enough. What really must be proven at this stage is whether people will hand over real money to buy your product. Or, to use a common business term, we are looking for "product market fit." What we mean by this is that it solves a clear problem for a customer, it can actually be made and delivered, and it can be produced at a price point that makes business sense.

With our cookstove example, there are plenty of ways that we can try to find our product market fit. Hypothetically, we've decided to work hard as a team for a fortnight on this challenge. Given we have five customer segments, we will spend a day on each of them in week one, and give them all a second day in week two. Let's imagine we did the activities below and had the following results:

Homeowners: We loaned our cookstoves to 20 families who we thought were our bullseye customers in this market segment (lower income, cooking their own basic dishes). At the end of the week, we returned to collect the stoves and capture feedback, but also to see if the households wanted to keep the new stove. Interestingly, four of the 20 families decided to purchase their stoves, and another three asked if they could pay it off in installments. That's a win; homeowners may be a key customer segment for us!

Restaurants: We gave the same trial option to 10 restaurants in our community. All were small and making simple local cuisine (tea and donuts for breakfast, stews and flatbreads for lunch). Unfortunately, when we went back to collect them, and see if they wanted to buy, no-one took us up on the offer. They said that the stoves didn't manage the volume they needed for the restaurant, but two restaurant owners asked to buy a cooker for their home, which was again a win for the homeowner market segment.

Wholesale shops: Rather than just walking into a store, we tried to get meetings with the purchasers who make the decisions for these stores. We were unable to do so, but we did draw on connections to find out who these buyers were and will keep trying over the coming month.

Non-Profit Organizations: We emailed friends at some non-profits to see if they would be interested in purchasing the stoves, and they said that the contracts for these kinds of products are usually three years long and most were not up for renewal any time soon. We were able to get through to World Vision's innovation team, and they have asked us to send them a stove to look at, which we did. We will follow up with them in a week.

Weekend Campers: We realized that we have no contacts at all in the weekend camper market, so we just emailed a few camping stores and magazines but had no response. We decided to stop pursuing that market segment.

Based on our two-week market validation sprint, while we are not fully done yet, we have enough to know that we will tailor our product for the homeowner market and push to try to get our stoves into wholesalers to sell in their stores. Our radical customer segment (the one we are not sure about but are still curious about) is the non-profit market.

We think this is enough to move to the next stage of the journey.

Make sure you spend some time doing your own market validation for your products or services.

To recap:

In this step of the journey, you:
- determined what kind of business model you have;
- looked at your unit economics;
- worked through a business model canvas; and
- looked at your market validation.

CHAPTER 7

We'll cover the next stage in just a few pages, but you'll be making some very important decisions that will alter much of the next decade of your life.

It's time to figure out if you are going to launch this business or not!

1. It is unacceptable that ✓
2. We believe ✓
3. But right now the reality is that ✓
4. The root cause we are going to focus on is ✓
5. The ideas ✓
6. Test the best ✓
7. Does it help to solve the problem in a scalable and sustainable way? ✓

Chapter 8

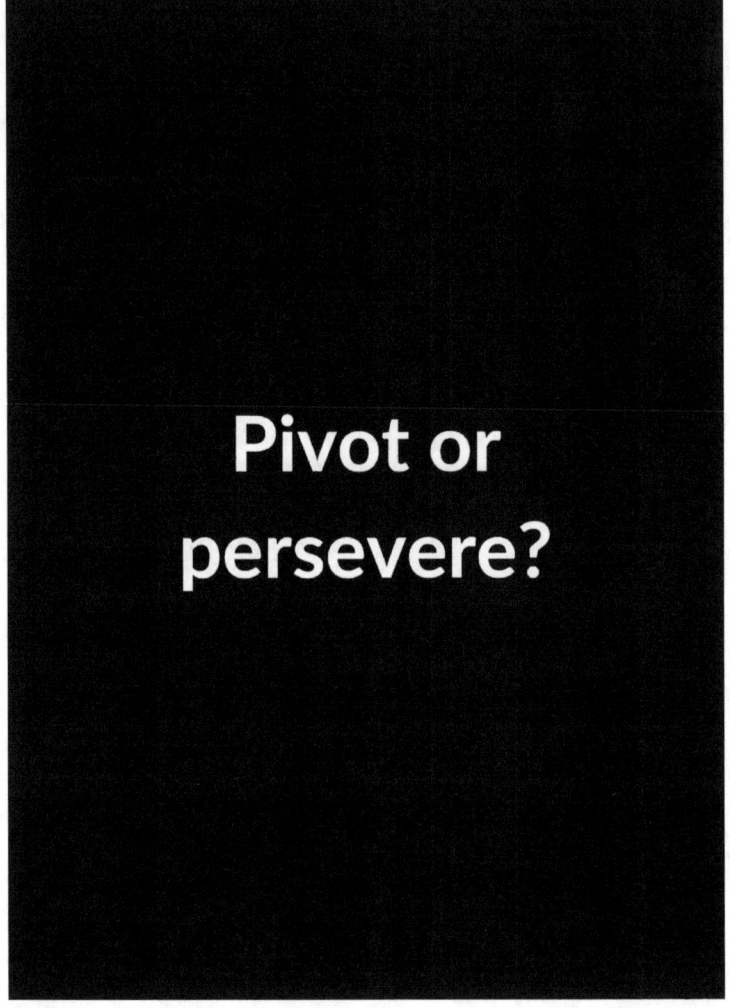

Seven.

As we mentioned at the start of the book, that's the number of years you need to think about.

CHAPTER 8

Are you willing to commit seven years of your life to this business?

Seven years of the anxiety that comes with looking through the financial statements and trying to balance your budget each month.

Seven years of sometimes having to be the bad boss and disappoint your team.

Seven years of those moments of frustration that keep us up at night when a customer leaves a bad review.

Seven years of being told NO plenty of times.

Of course, it's not all bad news; there are going to be plenty of great times in those seven years as well! But, overall, building a business is a grind.

During this chapter, you need to truly confront the big decision of whether you will commit a large part of your life, money, and effort for the next seven years to this business you have innovated.

Why seven years?

We've met plenty of entrepreneurs who think that their idea will take off after a year or two, and they will either hire a team to run everything for them, or they can sell and hit the jackpot.

It's easy to be inspired by the unicorns of Silicon Valley (like the YouTubes or the Instagrams which quickly rocketed to billion-dollar valuations). But it is important to remember that they are called unicorns for a reason – it's fantasy land. Such businesses rarely emerge.

More realistically, here is what we usually see happen.

Years 1 and 2: It might just be you, or, if you are lucky, a co-founder too. You will work incredibly hard for sales. You will ship product that in the future you will look back upon and laugh about. When your first customers buy your product, you will be excited, wonder if they "really" want it, and be curious to learn about how they came across you. If you can pay yourself any kind of salary, even a day or two a week, that's a big win. You will be working out of home, or a desk at a friend's office, or, if you really want to splurge and spend your hard-earned income, at a co-working space (make the most of the free drinks on Friday!).

Years 3 and 4: Sales have usually started to pick up by this point (if not, you've probably got a problem). You will likely be paying yourself now and have the beginnings of your office/shop or warehouse. You will likely be paying other people as well. Balancing the financial books each month becomes more complex and, as a boss, there is a growing anxiety that comes with this. More and more people know your company, but you are still excited and surprised when you bump into people with your product or service. You may be at the point where you can raise capital to expand if this makes sense for your business model.

Years 5 and 6: It's become very normal now for you to run this business. You have a small- to medium-sized team of people who help to keep things going, but you face the normal challenges of keeping them committed. You certainly have some classic products that people love purchasing, put you also keep innovating new ideas. By this point, things can start to be less inspiring and exciting for you unless you keep true to the core of the problem you are trying to solve. You are not likely to be rich, but there is income, maybe even profit, and you are continuing to grow.

The seven-year itch and beyond: If you have survived to this point, you are likely to have a profitable business. As the founder, you will either want to keep running everything for the rest of your working life (often called a lifestyle business), or you are getting bored and may want to start your next thing. Sustainability and sale are the key words here, meaning you either want to get the business to run well without you needing to do everything, or you are interested in getting out of the business (by selling it to a competitor, your employees, or investors). While the latter may be tempting, it's a rare outcome for many businesses, so be careful not to assume that this will happen easily.

While the first seven years don't always play out like this, and you may be the rare unicorn exception, it's a good reality to keep in mind. As we stressed early in the book, you still have time to decide if this is really what you want for the next seven years of your life. It is fine to make the brave decision that maybe this is not the right business, that being an entrepreneur is not right for you, or the timing is not right. Some things to look out for in support of this are:

1. Your heart is no longer in it: For some reason the passion is gone, and the idea no longer excites you. It's good to know this now, because a few years into the entrepreneurial journey this happens to all of us, where even the most inspired ideas can lose their luster. If you are feeling uninspired in the first weeks and months of your project, the chances are that things are not going to get any better, so it may be wise to close up shop early. Make sure, though, that you don't confuse discouragement with a lack of inspiration. We all get told no plenty of times in the early days of a business, and it takes grit to push through that.

2. Your personal situation doesn't allow for it: Make sure you can realistically afford to take the financial risk that comes with being an entrepreneur. For example, if you are thinking of starting a family (we've been there), or you need to focus on your health, or help a family member, this may not be the right time for your business. Your health, your family's wellbeing, and your personal relationships are incredibly important, more important than the business you are thinking about starting!

3. The numbers just aren't making sense: If you've gone through your unit economics, done a bunch of tests, and things are still not looking like they will work, you need to stop kidding yourself and realize that maybe this idea is a dud. Do the realities of being an entrepreneur work financially for you (e.g., if you are paying off debt, or trying to buy your first home, this may set you back a few years). Don't ignore the warning signs we've highlighted throughout this book, and if things

still aren't working, either pause the business for now or make some bold changes to the business model.

We will ask this just one more time.

Do you want to buckle into this wild ride for at least seven years?

Of course, the business model will change slightly over time, but, essentially, this is the thing that will define the next decade of your life, and as entrepreneurs we only have so many swings at launching and really trying with a business.

Don't forget about your personal situation here. If you are planning to have a family in the coming years, how will this tie in?

Now for the positive!

The flipside, which we also talked about earlier in the book, is that these seven years will also be amazing. You will likely feel more fulfilled than you would have been if you were working for someone else. You will have highs and lows but, as the saying goes, riding the rollercoaster is more exciting than riding the merry-go-round. If you can move through to profitability, depending on your business model, you could do very well financially. Most importantly, if the business makes a difference, you will always know that you did something that really mattered.

Ultimately, the decision is yours. Live deliberately, and boldly choose what you want for your life.

Otherwise, others will choose for you.

We chose the entrepreneur route and have never regretted it.

We've been lucky to do well financially.

We've made a difference.

How to fail gracefully

If you've determined that this idea is not going to work, then it's time to shut up shop.

Now, the good news at this point is, as we've mentioned a few times, there isn't much of an operation going on, so closing is often easy. Here are the things to think about:

- Leftover Stock: How can you get rid of physical stock in a way that is good for the world and make some money while you are at it? For example, if you have clothing, put up a bunch of signs around town and do a popup sale. If it is food, set up at the local markets, make a dish that will be popular, and try to clear through it all in a day or two.

- Existing Costs: If you are paying for a website you are no longer using, or a corner of a warehouse you don't need, or Facebook ads that are leading nowhere, cancel all these as quickly as you can. If you've decided to close the business, you won't have any revenue to cover those costs, so shut them down as fast as possible.

- Investors: You shouldn't have had any investors this early, so this shouldn't be a problem. If you have made an error and got investors onboard this early, you are going to need to take a close look through those deals you signed, and then start having tough conversations with them. To do the right thing, if there is any money you can claw back from selling stock, or if you have any money in the bank, pay them back before you pay yourself anything.

- Community: If you have engaged a whole bunch of people and they are relying on your products already (again, unlikely to be the case this early), then you need to let them know that things will be closing. If you just have a list of email subscribers who were semi-interested in your product, then shoot them an email to tell them the party is over. Chances are they might delete the email without a second thought and move on with their lives (I know, hard to hear such brutal honesty!). Still, take the time to craft a message and do your best to look after your early community. Of course if you feel you don't need to share it with anyone, that's fine too!

What can you learn through a failure?

These last few pages might appear a little depressing at first, but rather than viewing this decision to ditch your idea as a failure, see it as a big learning opportunity!

Take the time to sit down and truly engage with the question of what you have learned from this fail.

What was that breakthrough moment that you can bring into the next business? For example, you might now realize that instead of selling a low-priced product in high quantities, there are better returns in higher-priced products at lower quantities. Or you may have realized that your target market was wrong and have discovered a far more lucrative demographic of people that you think will buy the next product that you dream up. Or you might have learned a whole bunch about having a product manufactured or about how to do online advertising.

What did you learn about yourself? Did you learn that you are awesome at sales, but really need to learn more about financial book-keeping? Or were you a great creative who could come up with product fast, but needed someone to help you turn it into a viable business?

These are all useful insights to know about yourself, so that in your next business idea, you are better prepared to find the right people to partner with. So be prepared to ask the tough questions and bring those learnings forward with you, because if you fail to face them head on, you might repeat them!

Pulling up your socks and going again

It's important to note that if you've decided things aren't working out with this idea and to call it quits, you don't necessarily need to go right back to the drawing board.

Instead, maybe you just need to go back to step seven of the journey and ask some questions around whether the idea solved the problem in a scalable and sustainable way. Are there tweaks you could make at that point that would make your offering more compelling?

Or could you go back to steps five or six and test a few of your other ideas out (you might have 48 or so available if you did your homework!).

If you still haven't found something worth pursuing at this point, bounce back to step four and figure out if you really circled the right root cause.

Or you can go back even further and make sure you had a good grasp on the current reality.

Or, if that hasn't worked for you, then you've truly arrived back at the start, asking yourself the big question of what you are passionate about, and whether you want to be an impact entrepreneur that wants to launch a business that makes a difference.

Feel free to move backwards and forwards like this through your journey. If things aren't feeling great, take a breath, dust yourself off, figure out where you are on the journey, and then, if you want to be an entrepreneur that changes lives, get up and get moving again!

Please don't become the entrepreneur who fails once and then spends the next few years speaking at events about failure and how important it was for them. Sure, it's great to acknowledge that entrepreneurship is hard, but we don't need you dwelling on that; the world needs you to think up your next idea.

Aaaaand if it did work, it's time to build this business!

If you've read through all of that, feel like none of it applies to you, and you are fully convinced that you are on to something great with this business idea, that is awesome! It's a thrilling feeling, isn't it?!

To recap, this means you feel like you have green lights on the following:
 - You are inspired and ready to make something of this.
 - Your testing went well, and people bought what you are selling.
 - Your unit economics work and this could make a profit.
 - The idea has the potential to make the impact you are hoping it will.
 - You have the beginnings of a business model canvas.

It's starting to get serious.

CHAPTER 8

1. It is unacceptable that ✓
2. We believe ✓
3. But right now the reality is that ✓
4. The root cause we are going to focus on is ✓
5. The ideas ✓
6. Test the best ✓
7. Does it help to solve the problem in a scalable and sustainable way? ✓
8. Pivot or persevere? ✓

Chapter 9

CHAPTER 9

Turn your test into a real product

Up to this point, everything you have being doing can be summed up as "experimenting" and "playing with hypotheticals." Now it's time to turn all your insights into a product that is both scalable and sustainable. What we mean by this is:

Scalable: You now know how to make and sell one unit of your product or service, which is awesome. But can you realistically sell and deliver 10, 100, 100,000 of those same things? Obviously, selling at different levels like this brings different challenges and opportunities, but you now need to start thinking of whether you can operate with such quantities.

Sustainable: Again, you know how to sell one unit of your product or service and have proven that through your testing phase. But can you keep doing that over and over? For example, if you own an olive grove, and you've used all your olives for the year to make olive oil at certain price, you probably can't make them at that price again until another annual season comes around. Or if you have just produced an incredible music festival, but it wore you and your team out so much that you don't think you can do it again, then you have an issue. It's important to spend some time thinking how your idea can be repeatable, meaning it is relatively easy for your company to do what you do, over and over again.

There are some things you can do to make your business more scalable and sustainable.

Outsourcing

You don't need to do everything yourself.

In fact, you can't.

But you can outsource different parts of your business.

For example, let's say you manufacture clothes.

If you are not the source of creativity for your fashion label, you could hire a creative consultant to design your clothing range. Rather than setting up your own factory and starting to sew, you could source your fabrics from several different places and then have them sewed at another factory (or several factories). You could have a graphic designer come up with your packaging and have it printed by a commercial printer. Your job in all of this might be the project manager and the salesperson, but you are no longer doing much of the hands-on work with the actual making of the product.

Outsourcing can be extended to accounting, legal, customer service, returns system ... the sky is the limit, really. It's worth asking yourself what you can outsource, and what do you want to keep in-house so that you have a full control on quality? Consignment centers can also do the hard work of storing, packaging, and posting your products, so you engage very little in getting an item to your customer when a sale is made.

Remember, though, all this outsourcing is going to alter your unit economics!

Fewer options

There can be a tendency at this stage to get really excited and start to come up with loads of different product options. This confidence can be fueled by the success of your testing round, thinking you have the "Midas touch" and that everything you produce will be a hit.

It's really important, however, to not get carried away and keep your product options to a minimum. You are on to a winning idea, so don't overwhelm people with too much choice too early. Often, when people see too many products on offer, they become overwhelmed and choose to shop elsewhere. It is commonly believed that people will buy more of a product on a grocery shelf if there are less options to choose from. If you analyze the films that have won the Oscar for best picture in the last 20 years, almost all of them have also at least been nominated for the best film editing category. Quite simply, the more successful films are also good at editing things out. Doing more, with less.

Boxing it up

Now is the time to determine EXACTLY what is in your product or service. Remember that every little thing you add in or remove will have an impact on your finances and time, so it's vital to be crystal clear on this now.

Let's look at a company we've mentioned already in this book, Free to Feed (F2F). As a reminder, they employ refugees and asylum seekers to run cooking classes for customers. When deciding what their product will look like, they need to determine:

- Does F2F run the cooking class at customers' homes or in its own space?
    - At a F2F class, do you get one chef to train customers, or several?
        - Does F2F bring all the cooking equipment (i.e., knives, pots,

etc.) or do they expect customers to provide these?

- Do F2F bring all the ingredients (like oil, salt, pepper, etc.), or is it expected customers have some of these themselves?

- Does F2F bring drinks for people, or is that something the customer organizes?

- Do the customers receive gifts they can keep at the end of the experience?

As you can see, there are lots of decisions to be made, and, of course, a price has to be set as well. We've covered a lot of these financial decisions in previous chapters, but what we are saying here is that it is important to be clear on what makes up your product line and start marketing that exact product line now. Stay focused here.

Authority to operate

Many entrepreneurs might find the last part of this chapter is a little boring, so we will keep it short.

But it's super important, so read carefully!

Make sure you are allowed to be doing what you are doing.

To start with, that means being registered as a business in your country or state.

Beyond this, you need to determine the licenses, registrations, or authority you need to do what you do.

For example, if you are marketing fair-trade coffee, you need to have the fair-trade certification. You will also most likely need to have the food health authority registrations approved. If you are exporting, you may need licenses for that.

The easiest way to learn about these required certifications is to ask someone in your industry (perhaps not someone who is a direct competitor) about your legal obligations. Now, the easy thing, of course, is to fly under the radar and not do these things, as many startup entrepreneurs do, but be warned it could catch up with you at some point! We also know that getting these registrations is much easier in some countries than others. We've had to register businesses in many countries around the world and can empathize with those of you that have to face very slow and bureaucratic (and, unfortunately, sometimes corrupt) governments.

Now, let's look at what it takes to turn your product into a company.

CHAPTER 9

1. It is unaccceptable that ✓
2. We believe ✓
3. But right now the reality is that ✓
4. The root cause we are going to focus on is ✓
5. The ideas ✓
6. Test the best ✓
7. Does it help to solve the problem in a scalable and sustainable way? ✓
8. Pivot or persevere? ✓
9. Turn your test into a real product ✓

10

Chapter 10

CHAPTER 10

Turn your product into a company

Starting a company is a big deal, and a major responsibility.

If all goes well, at some point you will be paying people's salaries – which means they can eat, live in a house, and buy nice things for themselves, because of something you created. You may be reporting to investors who have put their money into your idea. You will be paying tax to the government, signing contracts with suppliers, keeping customers happy, paying the rent, balancing the books, and, overall, having to be a very responsible adult!

In this chapter, we try to detail a bunch of the things that you will need to think about to run your company effectively. Starting with some legal questions.

How are you going to be structured?

That's a big question for an impact entrepreneur.

Usually, for a regular company, you would just register as a business. But with the impact approach, you have options.

We've mentioned them earlier in the book, but let's talk through them again, this time with your business structure in mind.

Firstly, and most traditionally, you could be a non-profit.

Don't worry too much about the other titles that are floating around (e.g., charity, NGO, NPO, social enterprise, etc.). What you are really looking for here is the non-profit legal structure. This will be a type of organizational registration with your government. There are plenty of benefits to being a non-profit. For example, you may be able to minimize your tax bill, or not pay any tax at all. You may also be able to access grant funding (where foundations or donor organizations gift your company money to support your work) or donations from people. There is official reporting to government that comes with being a non-profit, and you are also likely to need to appoint an independent board which ultimately has power over the organization (including the power to fire you one day if they feel this is appropriate!). You are very unlikely to get rich running a non-profit, which might suit you perfectly if making money isn't your primary goal. But it is worth thinking about the future here. For example, if you plan at some point to start a family or put some money away for retirement, then you may wish you had prepared for this earlier. We've been involved with non-profits for years: starting them, running them, sitting on the boards of them, and even moving on from them when our time was done.

Alternatively, you could be a for-profit business. In a for-profit business you will have owners (with shares), which will likely be you and any co-founders. You will register as a business with your government, and, as revenues start coming in, you will have tax bills that you will need to pay. You are not likely to access grant funding or donations and instead will structure your company to rely more on the sales of your goods or services. In such a business, particularly in the early days, you can operate a lot faster and leaner because you don't have to wait several months for a board to sign off on your next moves. You can also structure your profits how you like, and use these to make an impact if you choose. For example, if your business has an after-tax profit of US$100,000 at the end of the year, you can do a few things:

- You could invest it back into the business to help you grow.

- You could donate it to a cause you believe in (for example, Who Gives a Crap, the toilet paper company we mentioned earlier, donates 50% of its profits to building toilets).
- You could reward the owners as you feel that your business has already made a significant difference that year through its products and services. If you owned 50% of the company, you would therefore receive US$50,000, which is great!

We've run both non-profits and for-profits.

In our 20s we were all about non-profits; but to be honest, in our 30s, as we had a family and felt like we needed to set ourselves up financially, we've leaned towards for-profit structures. The for-profit businesses still make a difference (in fact, maybe arguably even more of a difference than non-profits we started), but we also make money for our family which pays for our house and our children's school fees. What we do in our 40s and 50s remains to be seen.

Founders

This one word is almost always charged with emotion, ego, opportunity, and challenges, which is important to unpack.

We would recommend starting a business or organization with a great co-founder. You can try to go it alone, but it is like one-hand clapping (it is hard to make a lot of noise and you are going to get tired quickly). A co-founder is a companion on your journey who can pick you up if you are down (something you will, of course, have to do for them as well).

Having a co-founder also doubles your firepower in the important early years of the business, and if you can find someone who is strong where you are weak it can help to fill some big capacity gaps early on. Practically, what we mean by this is that if you are a brilliant salesperson but terrible at managing operations, you are going to need someone to deliver the business' products while you sell them. Or if one of you is creative and designs the products but the other person can bring them into the world, that is also going to be very useful.

We often find that the best co-founder relationships we have had are where we are having disagreements on ideas and challenging each other on strategy. If you have started this company with your best friend, and you are so alike that you agree on everything and bring the same skills and beliefs, then potentially one of you is not needed. Consider differentiating your roles early on, and investing in developing your respective responsibilities (for example, one of you could build up your skills in marketing and the other on logistics). By all means, launch a business with your friend; just make sure you are bringing double the value with two of you there.

If you have plenty of great ideas for a technology company and an excellent eye for marketing but can't write a line of code to save your life, you are going to need to find a co-founder who knows about technology. You may be OK with just some basic web support if you want to run a simple e-commerce site with off-the-shelf products, but if it is anything more than this, then you ABSOLUTELY must have tech talent in your founding team! You will need to spend time in technology communities to find someone with these skills, so look around in your town for meetups, pitching competitions, and hackathons that are populated with lots of techies.

If your business is in a specific sector (like education, agriculture, or fashion), and you don't have a wealth of experience in that line of work, it makes sense to go out and find a co-founder who can bring that to the table. For example, my (Aaron's) co-founder for an education company was Dave Faulkner, an award-winning teacher and school principal. Together, we fused our ideas to create something successful.

We have also found over the years that sometimes it is easier if your co-founder isn't your best friend. This means you don't have to hang out on weekends, like the same music, enjoy the same kinds of restaurants, or have the same fashion sense. If you can keep your co-founder relationship focused on the business, you will find it easier to make the tough calls you are going to need to make over the years without personal friendship dynamics getting in the way.

Similarly, if your co-founder is your romantic partner, be warned that, in our experience, this is risky. We were co-founders of our first non-profit, and while there were some amazing moments, there were some tough times as well. A few years after founding our first non-profit Spark we had to have a proper sit down and reassert that our relationship was more important than the organization. Looking back, it is crazy to think that it took us three years to make this clear. We ended up rewriting our job descriptions, moved into working on different parts of the business (rather than being in each other's pockets every day), and ensured that neither of us was more senior than the other. We also ensured that we didn't talk about work on Sundays, in the bedroom, or after 9:00pm. Sometimes these rules worked; other times they didn't. Of course, we look back on what we built together and are proud, but to be honest neither of us are rushing into running a business together again any time soon. There is another practical reason why starting a business with your life partner is not always a great idea. If the business goes through a rough patch and you are unable to pay yourself, it is helpful if another person in your house is still earning money!

With your co-founder, it's important to determine clear job titles early on. Importantly, one of you needs to be the CEO. We see some people trialing co-CEO arrangements, but we are not fans of these. Instead, we would recommend that you figure out who as CEO is going to be up at night thinking about cashflow, risk, and strategy, freeing up the other person to be the revolutionary creative, or the passionate salesperson, or the lead on whatever roles you deem most important. While your job descriptions will quickly adapt as the business grows, make sure that they are written down early, and that they are guiding your activities.

Also know that arguments between co-founders are very normal; in fact, we would encourage them if they are around product or strategy. The more you can talk vigorously through your ideas and view a problem from different angles, the better. Importantly, practice "being frank and then rallying." This means that you are honest, and even aggressive, in sticking up for an idea, but then once a decision is made, know that you made it together and that you will do your best to make it happen. Once you rally behind an idea, a person should never say, "I told you that was never going to work!" Of course, you should always present as a united team in front of clients, donors, or partners; leave your arguments behind closed doors!

It's really important that you invest in your co-founder relationship. If things are broken, be quick to fix them. Have tough conversations. Go away on company retreats out of town where you can think and strategize. Buy each other birthday presents. Keep an eye on each other's wellbeing. Be aware, to a certain extent, of their personal life and when they may need space or support, but don't get too involved!

Finally, the sticky topic of founders and shares.

If you are registered as a non-profit, then this makes things very easy, because there are no shares to split up. But if you are a for-profit business, there are shares to consider. If both founders started the company together, then the simplest approach is 50% each to begin with. If one person had the idea and started everything first, then, maybe they get more (e.g., a 60/40 split). Or perhaps it is clear that one person is going to be doing more work, and the other more experienced person is lending their support part-time. Maybe here there would be a 70/30 split, or 80/20. In the early days, things can feel nice and simple with the business and shares, but know that soon you may have to start to give up some of those shares to investors if you are looking to raise money, or employees if you choose to have a scheme where you give shares out alongside their salary packages. This means you may want to set aside some shares, or you may want to restructure your ownership at this point (remembering all these steps need lawyers, who cost money!) Another thing to think about is the concept of "vested shares." These reward employees for their time spent in the company. Let's say you bring in a "co-founder" a few years after you have started. Perhaps at their first-year anniversary they get 5% of the company. At the two-year mark, that kicks up to 12%, and then at year three they settle at 17%. This may be a better way to do things, rather than running the risk of you giving away 50% of the shares to someone only to see them walk away after six-months (ouch).

But where can you find a co-founder if you don't already have one?

Realistically, there may be someone you already know who is living a good life in a company or running their own business, and you need to convince them that they should be involved in your amazing new thing. This is hard to do, but if the idea is compelling, it should make your job easier. The other place to find co-founders is at industry-specific meetups, boot camps, hackathon weekends, and all the other startup style events in your town or online.

Good luck finding the right person if you haven't yet, and good luck with your co-founder relationship when you do discover Mr. or Mrs. Right!

Now let's move to how you can bring early cash into your business.

1. It is unacceptable that ✓
2. We believe ✓
3. But right now the reality is that ✓
4. The root cause we are going to focus on is ✓
5. The ideas ✓
6. Test the best ✓
7. Does it help to solve the problem in a scalable and sustainable way? ✓
8. Pivot or persevere? ✓
9. Turn your test into a real product ✓
10. Turn your product into a company ✓

Chapter 11

Raising money

Let's talk money (that doesn't come from selling your products and services), and how you can bring it into your business.

We'll look at fundraising in a charitable sense first, which is where high net worth individuals (people with money), or foundations, essentially gift money to your organization. This is likely to only be something that you will do if you are a non-profit.

When you fundraise, you are not just raising a general sum of money; rather, you are trying to achieve very specific goals. For example, let's say you were starting a school in your community. You know you need around US$1 million to secure the land, train the staff, and open and run the school for the first two years. What you would do here is itemize exactly what you need and try to get a whole bunch of it for free (e.g., are there people who will volunteer to train the teachers, can someone gift you the land, can a graphic designer do your branding for free, can a technology company donate computers?). Then, where you need to raise money, you would target the amounts you need. For example, if you were invited to speak at a three-day philanthropy conference, you might go in with a number one goal of raising US$100,000. This would see you having as many meetings as possible, networking with as many people as you can, and even boldly asking for that amount from the stage! To achieve this, you would have to do some professional stalking, where you find out who is attending, and then be bold enough to try to meet for coffees, or walk up to people at conference drinks and introduce yourself (because you have googled what they look like). You might have a one-in-a-thousand hit rate, but your goal is to find that person who can get you the US$100,000. I (Aaron) once had 73 meetings in four days during a major conference in New Delhi with one very specific goal: determining if we would launch in India, and if so with whom would we partner. We didn't end up launching in India, but in Bangladesh instead!

Philanthropy 101

The word "philanthropist" comes from the Greek, and it means essentially a "love for humanity."

The idea of philanthropy is that people are eager to improve the lives of others, or the world in some way, and can be convinced (or already have a strong compulsion) to give money to your cause.

A good way to think about who you might approach to fundraise money like this is by looking at the three Cs, which we learned from our friends at the social accelerator Uncharted: capacity, care, and connection.

Firstly, you are looking for a donor who has the CAPACITY to support you. Basically, this means they have money available to give you. Specifically, it means that they have the cash available at the time you need it. There are plenty of people who appear wealthy, with a nice big house or a fancy car, but they may have a great deal of debt, or spend every cent they earn, or are having a bad year where they are not able or willing to give. These are not your people. Rather, if you can, you should be trying to find out which foundations are gifting good amounts of money, or which families and individuals are regularly giving to causes each year. Once you have a sense of what amounts people or groups are giving, you need to tailor your request accordingly. For example, if the smallest gift a foundation gives is US$5 million then asking for

US$25,000 for your startup organization will likely not go well for you. Equally, if you approach a philanthropic family who give around US$10,000 a year, then they may be embarrassed or turned off by a request for US$1 million.

Many foundations and high net worth donors give at similar times each year. It can therefore be useful to build up a calendar of when possible grant applications close each year, or when donors most often make their decisions (big tip: it usually has a lot to do with when taxes are due in their country). On the point of tax, if you want to take grants from philanthropic sources, make sure that you have the right legal and tax registrations to allow people to give money to your non-profit organization as a tax-deductible gift. It's always disappointing when someone wants to donate to your cause, but they can't because of the way you are structured, or because you can't offer the tax exemption status that they require.

The second C is that you need to find people who CARE about your cause. If a well-off family or foundation is focused on donating to cancer charities, for example, they likely have a very compelling reason for this (perhaps someone in their family who was very important passed away from cancer). It is therefore going to be a very tough sell to try to convince them that this year they should direct 25% of their giving to your organization which is focused on supporting children to read. Make things easier for yourself and focus your efforts on people who seem to be very interested in your cause. You can ask similar groups to you for this information from (they may not always give it though, people are likely to be competitive!), or you could even be cheeky and look at their websites or annual reports to see who is funding them. You should be well prepared to accept that the list of foundations and families who are passionate about your specific cause may be small.

Bear in mind that as philanthropists gain more experience, they often become more sophisticated and end up becoming very niche in their work. Once they have their "thing" that they like to fund, it can be hard to convince them otherwise. Also, many people wrongfully assume that because businesses (as opposed to foundations) have plenty of money that they are easy to get donations from. The unfortunate reality that we and many impact entrepreneurs have experienced is that the number one goal of many companies is often to make money for their shareholders (which in many countries is their legal responsibility). While there are some "good" companies which are very generous, or perhaps they are registered as a B Corp, for most profit is the biggest priority. Therefore, if you can help them make more money by partnering with you, you may have a shot; but if this is a pure loss-making activity for them, you might find it hard to have them return your emails! It's possible, and we've done it many times, but sometimes it can be more trouble than it's worth.

Finally, people tend to give to a cause if they know someone involved, hence the third C is CONNECTION. If you send a cold email to the "contact us" page of a foundation, you should be very surprised if you get a reply. Instead, what you want is a warm introduction from someone who is closely connected to that group. Or, if you can get yourself into the circles where these people are spending time (say, at relevant conferences or events), or even be asked to sit on panels at these events with them, then you really increase your chances of opening a door. One thing you could also consider is asking philanthropists to mentor you or join your board. This isn't done in a manipulative way; instead, you are genuinely interested in learning from their success and their insights, and if they decide to donate to your organization, or give you access to their network, well, that's a win!

If you find that a meeting with a philanthropist isn't going well (for example, they like donating to cat rescue shelters not aspiring basketball players from challenging communities in Los Angeles like you had hoped), then try to salvage something from the meeting by asking them if they have any people they think you should meet, or at the very least have them leave thinking that you are a lovely person. Remember that word spreads. Philanthropists speak to each other; in fact, there is usually only a few degrees of separation between many networks in cities and countries. So be careful, because if bad rumors start spreading about you, that can be hard to repair.

Another way to build up your connections is to talk to people who work in your sector. For example, if you work in clean water, you could engage with the local government, other charities, or companies which support clean water programs and simply ask them, "Do you know of any groups which are funding innovative clean water projects like mine?" If you are struggling to find people to engage with your idea, you could also consider throwing an event yourself. Just make sure you are getting donors along in the hope of raising funding, rather than simply paying for a night of food and drinks for all your friends!

"Making the ask" of someone to donate their money to your organization is something that many people find very hard to do. If you want to raise philanthropic money, however, it is something that you will HAVE to get good at. You need to have the courage of your convictions that donating to your cause is the most powerful thing they can do with their money (and, if it isn't, then perhaps they should be writing that check for another group). If you are asking someone for funding in a meeting, be very clear and use strong language such as "we would love to partner with your family and see you support us with US$225,000 this year." If you don't ask as boldly as this, there's a good chance that someone else will get that funding. And be prepared to put your big girl/boy pants on, because you are likely going to be told no plenty of times.

When it comes to writing grant applications, know that there is a whole world of resources for this. Keeping things simple, we'd encourage you to do the following:

- Answer their questions. Every foundation has its own form that it likes, so don't just copy and paste answers from the last application you made.
- Be very explicit in how you will spend this funding if you are successful. Large chunks of funding for "admin" or "miscellaneous" costs are not going to fly.
- Only apply for grants where you meet most of the criteria they have set.
- Always think about opportunity cost – the profit you forego due to a lost opportunity. A good grant application could take you as much as five days to write. Is that a good use of your time, or should you have been dedicating that to other ways to find money?

CHAPTER 11

Beyond philanthropy

When you are thinking about fundraising, remember that it is not just about getting money from rich people! Perhaps you can secure free office or warehouse space for the next two years? Or maybe you can get a three-year supply of free coffee for your social enterprise café? Or maybe there are builders who will donate time to build your new store? Or perhaps a graphic designer or videographer will do free creative work for you? Or someone will donate catering to your next event? (These are all examples of things we have been able to secure). Money saved this way can instead be spent directly on your impact work.

You might want to think about selling a product to fundraise money for your cause. (Remember Socktober from earlier in the book? We ran that for a few years and raised about US$25,000!) Or you may look at running a fundraising campaign (something that we have been part of for years with our Polished Man campaign conceived by one of our co-founders, Elliot Costello). Without going into too much depth on fundraising campaigns, some things to think about are making sure: that it is easy for people to get involved with (where barriers to entry are low, like Red Nose Day); that it is conspicuous (where the word can spread easily, again like Red Nose Day); and that people can get their friends and family involved. For example, with the Polished Man campaign, men paint one fingernail and raise money during the month of October. We have seen other friends raise huge amounts with their "Do It in a Dress" campaign, where they get people to do dares in a dress to raise money for girls' education. And, of course, the world-famous ice-bucket challenge went on to raise hundreds of millions in aid of motor neuron disease ALS.

It's likely that, in the early days of your organization, you will not be raising millions of dollars; in fact, you will be lucky if you are able to raise tens of thousands. So, think big but start small and celebrate every donation, no matter how small.

Lastly on this point, the secret weapon for fundraising is to move people emotionally. If people are inspired, or deeply challenged by the cause you are raising for, then you have a chance. If you can't move them, they will think of five different ways to get out of giving you money! You must spend time thinking about the stories you can tell, picking those that will engage people emotionally and maybe even make them cry! Your cause matters; your job is to make it matter to them as well.

Raising investment

It is said that raising capital is a bit like dating as teenagers. Plenty of people are boasting about all the great things happening for them, but few are telling the truth!

If you go to an entrepreneurship meetup in your town, you will no doubt bump into people talking about all the Series As and venture capitalists (VCs) and angel investors that they are meeting with, but the number of actual deals being made is likely to be very low (unless you live in Silicon Valley!). Therefore, our goal in this short section is to break through the noise and talk about the basic things that you need to consider when raising capital from investors to finance the setup or growth of your business.

Our first tip is that you should try not to raise investment money.

Instead, try to focus on making the best kind of money, which is from sales of your products and services.

We personally think that too many companies spend too much time in their early years talking about and trying to raise investment, rather than just trying to sell their products and finance their growth slowly from money they are making. On top of this, while we know that this is very difficult for most to do, consider putting as much of your own money into the business as you can, by which we mean tapping into any savings you have, trading in your car or if you are really scraping things together selling some things from around your house (like clothes you haven't worn in a while!). If you read this and think, *I wouldn't put my own money into the business*, then the chances are you might struggle convince someone else to do the same.

While investment is not often talked about like this, it can be helpful to view a capital raise with the same level of excitement as getting approved for a credit card. Yes, you have access to money, but it's going to cost you a lot to service any debt you incur! For example, imagine you go out there and spend a year raising US$200,000. Congratulations! You then spend that money on a great new web developer, some online marketing, and a three-month lease on a new office. Poof, just like that it is gone! If you don't see a huge kick in revenue from that US$200,000 of investment, you have basically just set that money on fire and given away a chunk of your company at the same time, or found yourself in debt. So be very careful with the money you raise, and make sure you are using it in the way that you think will really help the company to grow.

If you are not convinced and feel that you absolutely must raise investment, that's fine too.

If so, there are a few different types of people you should be looking to engage with.

The first bunch are commonly referred to (with tongue in cheek) as the three Fs, which are your friends, your family, and fools. Your friends and family may send some money your way because they are excited by the idea and your enthusiasm. Fools, on the other hand, are people that you can convince this is a once-in-a-lifetime opportunity that they just have to be part of. Realistically, you might raise US$5,000 – US$25,000 from the three Fs, depending on where you live and who you know, and the most common time for this money to be raised is in your first year. At this stage, many people fall into the trap of having very little legal paperwork to support these investments (which can cause real problems later) or, because it is their first rodeo, end up giving away too much of their company to their second favorite aunty for too little cash. So, if you are raising this kind of money, bring in a lawyer who is familiar with startup laws, even at this early stage.

You might then move on to angel investors. These are often

people who have perhaps become well off through their own company, or maybe their parents gave them a big chunk of money (wouldn't that be nice!). Angel investors like to dabble in new ideas, they like the excitement of startup, or they get a thrill from engaging with enthusiastic founders. There are likely to be angel networks online, or in your town, or your sector, but usually the easiest way to find them is by investigating those who have previously invested in ventures like yours. Angels usually invest in a few specific sectors (like agriculture, education, health, etc.), so your aim is to find a match. An added bonus is if they have knowledge or connections around your industry, they can potentially open networks for you. Investment is often around the US$25,000 – US$100,000 mark, still in your first few years. Given angel investing is risky (only a small number of startups ever find themselves in a position to give a big return to an angel investor), they might demand a large chunk of your company for a small amount of money; but, unfortunately, that is the game you are playing here.

Often, angel investors will do these deals on a legal agreement called a "convertible note" or a "safe note," which is basically a shorter contract than that which would come with a full issuing of shares. Depending on the terms you draw up, there will be interest (i.e., the angel's investment grows in value each year); a conversion event (which is a point in time where you either raise with bigger investors or at the three-year mark); and also perhaps a discount rate (meaning the angels get a sweeter deal than the later investors in order to reward the risk they took early on). If you are considering this approach, you'll certainly want a startup savvy lawyer on your side to make sure you are not getting a bad deal. For now, you at least understand that these terms exist, and you'll know to learn more about them if you go down this route.

There is another path that is becoming more popular, known as revenue-based financing, where you pay off the investment as you make money through the business. You can also take on pure debt financing at this stage, which is where you go to a bank and ask for money. Walk into your nearest branch and ask to speak to a business banker, who will either be excited to see you or will tell you quickly that this is not an option for their bank, depending on the products they have available and the state of your business. If you are taking this option with a regular bank, be prepared for a very long period of paperwork. Unfortunately, depending on where you live, the collateral requirements and legalities around who can own property or open a bank account may mean that bank loans are inaccessible for many small business owners, women especially.

The next group you might want to talk to (usually two to five years into your company's history) is venture capitalists (VCs). VCs will be looking at investments of US$100,000 and upward. The way that VCs usually structure their business is that they raise a fund themselves and are therefore working to create a return for their own investors. They take their jobs very seriously because, well, they only get a worthwhile payday or repeat investors if they do a good job. VCs will likely do very thorough due diligence (expect this to take a few months at least), basically open-heart surgery on your company to figure out if you are a good investment or not. If you decide to move ahead and issue shares to a VC, they may want to sit on your board, and you will likely have to do some legal restructuring to prepare for the new allotment of stockholders. If you hear the term "Series A," it basically means the first big round of VCs investing in your company. Series B is the second and bigger round (and in turn Series C), but these are all big moments, and well beyond the startup phase of your business! If you are going down the VC route, know that these bigger players won't be impressed by the meetups you attend, the accelerators you have gone to, or the awards you have won. They will only be impressed by the fundamentals and the potential of your business, so in the early years, focus on growing the business rather than spending all your time in the "noise" that can sometimes define the startup community.

Below is a simple diagram of a common (but not the only) pathway to engage with different players throughout your investment journey. Remember, at each step you are selling more shares in your company, meaning less percentage for you (in the hope that you have a smaller slice of a bigger pie, rather than a big slice of a small pie).

Unfortunately, much of the advice on the topic of investment is written about the Silicon Valley experience. All the talk of unicorns (companies that grow to a billion-dollar valuation), and the legends of people like Mark Zuckerberg and Elon Musk, paints a rosy picture of a world that is often very far removed from the reality for most people. Unless you want to move to California and try to get into Y-Combinator (by all means go for it if that's your dream and you have a great tech idea), you should aim to approach investment with a healthy dose of reality. If you really want to raise capital in this way, then great, make it a priority. But if you believe there are other ways you want to grow your company, stop talking about "raising" and simply get to work with your own strategy.

The final thing to touch on with raising investment is that once you start down this track, you need to know that your investors will want their money back at some point. What this means is that they will want to see an exit where:

a) they sell their shares at a later stage raise to a new investor (rare);

b) they get their money back when the entire company is sold to a buyer (even rarer); or

c) you list on the stock exchange of your country, and everyone gets a great payday (crazy rare).

So yes, with investment you will bring in money to grow, but you may also lose some control of your business, start the clock on a pathway to an exit, and be forced bring new people on to your board. If you still want to raise capital, then best of luck to you; but if you've decided to finance through sales and revenue, and perhaps grow a little slower, then that's nothing to be ashamed of (in fact, we think it is kind of great).

Finally, it's worth noting that there are plenty of new financing approaches being developed each year. Ask around your entrepreneurial ecosystem to see if there are new mechanisms you could consider using for your business!

1. It is unacceptable that ✓
2. We believe ✓
3. But right now the reality is that ✓
4. The root cause we are going to focus on is ✓
5. The ideas ✓
6. Test the best ✓
7. Does it help to solve the problem in a scalable and sustainable way? ✓
8. Pivot or persevere? ✓
9. Turn your test into a real product ✓
10. Turn your product into a company ✓
11. Raising money ✓

Chapter 12

Running the business

Now for a little "how to run your business" BootCamp.

Some of this chapter will feel relevant immediately, and some of it you might find comes into play a few years into your journey (where you may need to dust of your copy of this book or download it again). By all means, read it all now, but we'd suggest keeping notes and remembering to come back to these as new challenges and opportunities arise.

Let's start our rapid little business course with branding and marketing.

Branding and marketing

It might feel strange that we've left this topic for later in the book, but this is deliberate. So far, we've wanted you to focus on engaging with your strategy, your business model, and the actual heart of what product or service you are selling (and whether people want to buy it). If you've come this far, now it's time to build the brand that sits around this.

Your big goal with your brand is that it should appeal directly to your target customers. As you know well now, your product or service exists to solve a problem for them, so make sure when you work on your branding and marketing you think about what THEY will like, more than what you like.

Before you jump into selecting colors and fonts, have a good think here about your company and what it stands for. Are you safe and conservative, or edgy and interesting? Are you appealing to your local market or an international one? Are you young or old? Do you want to create a brand that speaks to the demographic you are working with or to the exact product you have created? Are you looking for something that is on trend right now or something that you want to last for a long time?

When you've analyzed who you are, you can start to bring together the pieces of your brand.

Your name

You are going to need a brand name.

This can be different to the registered business name, so don't feel trapped by what it says on your business license certificate. It can be handy to think about the following with your brand name:

1. Make sure it is easily googleable. We once started an organization called Spark. People seemed to like the story behind the brand once we told it to them, but we admit now that it was incredibly hard to find on Google! One of my (Aaron's) favorite bands when I was young was The Music, another name that is very hard to find online when you are searching for musicians! Try to come up with something unique, so if people search for you online you are easy to identify. You might think it is a great idea to name your new social enterprise bakery Sweet Cakes, but a quick look on Instagram, Facebook, and Google will tell you that plenty of people beat you to that one.

2. Keep the name short and memorable. Ideally, one word, and in a perfect world less than seven letters! Given pretty much every four- and five-letter website with a .com domain name is now taken, it can be a cheeky trick to invent a six- or seven-letter word that evokes what you do but is still unique

and easy to find. For example, one company we invested in is called Kandua. They are a skilled tradesperson search agency in South Africa, and the idea is that "if you can't do it yourself, we 'Kan Du' it for you!" So Kandua is a nice fit, they are easy to find online (and could secure kandua.com), it evokes their product or service, and they can really claim ownership over the brand name. A good test with a made-up name, though, is to tell some friends the name, and a day later see if they can recall it. If people can't remember your name, it sucks!

3. Some other handy rules are to avoid complex acronyms (like the BNCAAA), names that can be easily teased (just ask your friends at Friday drinks to come up with every possible way to make fun of it), your own names (unless you are famous), or names that are very "now" but won't age well (i.e., something with a generational name like "y-generation" or "millennial." And, of course, make sure your potential competitors haven't already taken the name!

If you do a proper name innovation round, try to come up with a list of 20 or so, and know that you will need to compromise in the end to find something that works. Make sure you have a good one from the start, as it is much easier than trying to change it a few years down the track (again, trust us on that one). Good luck!

Your tagline

Taglines or slogans quickly build your brand beyond just a name and help you to educate your customer. For example, the socially-conscious cleaning company Method has a tagline of, "Home cleaning products." TOMS, the clothing and shoe brand, is much broader but implies social change quickly with the tagline "We're in business to improve lives." Now, if you are Nike or Apple and are in a position to throw millions at marketing each year, by all means go for something like "Just Do It" or "Think Differently," but in the early days, our advice would be to keep it clear.

Your logo

You could go on Fiver.com and get this done for literally US$5. Or, like Pepsi recently did, you could spend tens of millions of dollars updating your logo (and changing only a few things for all that money). The golden rule with your logo is to keep things simple, and the easiest way to do this is to just have your company name with a nice font (Coca-Cola is good example). If you want an image to accompany your logo, keep this as simple as possible (like the Nike swoosh or Apple's apple).

Your colors

You will need to think about your brand colors early on as well. Again, try to keep this simple, with ideally no more than three main colors in your palette, keeping in mind how these work on dark and light backgrounds. You should also think about how you want to use images, relying more on either photos (color, black and white, or with a filter on them), cartoons, or icons.

Your fonts

You will also need to pick consistent header (for titles) and body copy (for main text) fonts for your logo and to use on websites, social media posts, brochures, labels, and everything else you physically print or push out online. If you go for a basic font that is widely accessible, it keeps things simple; but if you go for a fancier font, know that you will have to buy this to legally use it.

Your tone of voice

Your tone of voice is the way that you speak to your customers.

Here you need to decide if you are you fun and friendly (great for a bar, for example), or professional (probably more appropriate for a law firm), or inspiring (perhaps for an activist group). Once you nail down your tone of voice, write with this in mind for all your communications.

These very basic elements that we've raced through make up your brand. Once you have this figured out, it's important that you stick to it as best you can (at least until you do a rebrand or a refresh). You can spend a lot of money getting a brand made up by impressive design agency, but the reality is that this is not always wise for a startup. To achieve the first iteration of your brand, we would recommend doing a bunch of research online to see what you like (Pinterest and Behance are always good for this) and then finding a graphic designer through a website like Upwork or Behance. Or you could find an up-and-coming graphic designer in your town who could do this at an affordable rate for you. We would encourage you not to do this yourself unless you are particularly skilled in this area (and don't get your second cousin's girlfriend to do it either, unless they are also excellent!).

Once you have your brand, your job is to get it out there, everywhere! Print out T-shirts and wear them daily and to every business event you go to. Get stickers, posters, postcards, and banners made up and put them everywhere. These are all cheap to print and help to get your new image out into the market.

Your website

Your website should exist for one reason.

And that reason should be decided by you.

If you want people to buy your product or service through the site, then everything should be designed to support and encourage people to do that. If you want them to call you and make a booking, then everything should point to that.

Many people fall into the trap of trying to do too much with their website, so we always say that the best approach is to figure out exactly what you would most like people to do, and then design everything around achieving that.

CHAPTER 12

Your social media

Social media can be a positive force for your business, but equally for some products and services it can also be a huge waste of time.

To help you figure out where your business sits on this spectrum, ask yourself a simple question: Are your bullseye customers likely to find you on social media? Or could word of mouth, foot traffic past your physical shop (if you have one), strategic partnerships, or some other approach be more important? If you are finding that social media is not helping with sales or engagement, then be careful how much time and money you spend on it.

If you feel social media is important, treat it like a cocktail party. If you just walk in and yell your company name over the loud music every hour, you won't get much of a reaction. But if you walk into the party and start having conversations with people, sharing interesting things with them, and maybe even helping them to solve some of their problems, you might have a good night! It's the same with social media. When you are walking into the metaphorical social media cocktail party, don't just yell three times a week. Instead, have conversations, post interesting content, and solve your potential customers' problems! A handy rule of thumb is to post three times a week, firstly with something interesting for your community but not directly about your product, secondly with something directly involved with your product, and thirdly with a call to action (an event you want people to buy tickets for, a sale, etc.). It pays to be at the right cocktail party as well, so be clear about what platform(s) your customers use and focus your efforts there.

Traditional media

This is another way to gain exposure for your brand.

Ideally, in startup, you shouldn't be paying for TV, newspaper, or magazine spots. Instead, you should be trying to get your positive impact story profiled where you can. If you want to pursue this type of exposure, become friends with the media, specifically with those journalists who are writing stories about your sector (i.e., those specializing in women, or social business, or the environment, or education). Where you can, reach out to them directly and tell them about interesting things you are up to, or invite them to your events. If they, in turn, start publishing stories about you, it is free marketing!

You must remember, though, that as nice as journalists may be to you, don't fall into the trap of always seeing the media as your friend and trusted confidant! A nasty story about you will almost always get more views than a nice one, and for every kind-hearted journalist, they likely have two buddies who would love to get the next inside scoop (if you find yourself doing something wrong). If you do engage with the media, or are working through a challenging media situation, determine early on what your soundbites are (the things you want to stick to saying), and try as hard as you can to not deviate from those!

CHAPTER 12

Speaking in public about your business

As a founder, it can be worthwhile taking some time to become a highly effective public speaker. You can draw on this important skill to inspire and educate your internal team and your customer community as well as engage with potential donors, investors, or partners. Of course, there are entire books, courses, and associations (like Toastmasters) that will train you how to speak. As founders who have had to speak about our work on many stages around the world, we've drilled down to a few key points we think are most useful:

- Tell stories. It might be your story, or the story of a customer, or of someone who needs your help. When you tell stories you relax, you move people, and you are more likely to connect with your audience.

- Be sincere, be brief, and then be seated. By which we mean stand on stage, say something honest, and then get off the stage. If someone gives you a two-hour spot for a speech, tell them you will speak for 20 minutes and take 10 minutes of questions instead.

- If you are terrified of public speaking (one of us used to be), then don't give speeches but instead do Q&As on stage. You will likely be much more relaxed, can respond based on things you know about your own business, and won't be worried about trying to memorize lines!

- Build up your stump speech, by which we mean a basic set of stories, ideas, and soundbites that you can draw on for most public events. You may be surprised to know that most professional speakers don't create a new speech every time they get on stage, so don't feel like you need to either. Or you can think of these points as your greatest hits, just like a band may roll out at their concerts.

- Practice. The more you get on stage, the more comfortable you will become. And think to yourself that rather than giving a speech in these moments, you are sharing your vision; it's very different.

Networking

Lastly for this rapid marketing course, networking.

This is not about being a socialite and going to an event every night of the week but instead making sure that you know the people that you should know in your sector or your city or country. To be honest, we stopped going to 90% of industry events in our second year as entrepreneurs, only attending those where we knew the big hitters would be who could potentially help us get to the next level of impact and scale.

But how do you network effectively?

The answer is to focus on who you are trying to connect with, rather than just having a big network. Quality, not quantity.

Let's say you are at an event, and there is a big investor, buyer, or donor who you really want to connect with. If you can, get on stage at that event, be on a panel with them, or at the very least ask a brilliant question from the audience when it moves to Q&A. Your goal is to stand out from the hundreds of people in the crowd and stick in that person's mind, so try to squeeze in your name and your company but do it very quickly. After the formal part of the event there will often be a break, or drinks, or some opportunity to connect with that person. Make sure you use this time wisely. Most obviously, you need to pluck up the courage to walk over and talk to that person. But also know that you may only have a minute or two to connect before they are distracted, interrupted, or have to go, so quickly get to the point of why you are trying to connect.

A classic mistake people make with networking is that they fail to make a clear ask, that is actually compelling to the person they are talking to. You can avoid this by making sure there is some kind of win for the other person (i.e., they will make money, or sell more product, or be able to invest their money in a way they are hoping to).

So, try to move quickly to something like:
  - *"I'd love to send my deck to you as I think we fit in your investment criteria,"* or,
  - *"Who is the person in your team who looks at new investments?"* or,
  - *"I'd love to run an idea by you that I think can improve the way you are selling to parents. Can I buy you a coffee?"*

At most events, it is unlikely you will be able to seal any deals there and then, but what you are hoping for is that the person you are trying to network with finds you interesting, and you can get a second meeting, or they will engage with your email when you reach out. So, treat that meeting as just the start of the conversation, and then get smart about how you get that second meeting with them. We have had plenty of success with a template email for second meetings that goes like this:

Hi there Mary,

It was so great to meet you last night at the event at Impact Hub. I loved your thoughts on how many exciting companies are emerging in South Africa at the moment! I also love that SAB is taking such a leading role in investing in the next generation of businesses. As promised, I'd love to support your vision and am happy to volunteer as a mentor in your high-school program. (Here we have jogged Mary's memory, talked about her work, and offered to help.)

I would also love to follow up on the possibility of a catch-up to share a little more about what we do at Bright Start, and how we may be a perfect fit for your SAB Stars investment program. (Now we have a simple and clear ask.)

Would you be open to grabbing a 20-minute coffee (my shout of course!) at the Velo café, which is just near the SAB headquarters. Does 8:30am on Tuesday November 23 work for you? If not, please let me know a time that suits better, and I will happily move my schedule around. (We've suggested a very specific time, date, and place.)

Once again, thank you for your great ideas last night and hope to connect soon.

Together, for a better South Africa.

Jonty Nkosi
  Founder and CEO
  Bright Start Enterprises
  jonny@brightstartenterprises.com

Bright Start Enterprises is a Johannesburg-based social enterprise that launches small businesses that bring people out of poverty. If you want to hire a landscaping, office cleaning, or catering company please get in touch with us. So far, we have created 87 jobs, but with your help we can create even more!

(We include a short business bio as part of the email signature.)

Again, you will see in this email above that Jonty has reminded Mary of who he is, offered something to her, given her a specific time for a possible second meeting, and included some info about his company. We have found that the strike rate is high for a follow-up email like this.

Also, back yourself. Don't be afraid to hit up the biggest people in the most senior roles, knowing that many of them love supporting passionate entrepreneurs. But also know that sometimes it is not the big boss you need. For example, if you are a toilet company, you might not want to try to get a meeting with Bill Gates (he's probably quite busy), but you may want to try to get a meeting with the Gates' Foundations head of sanitation, or the Gates' Foundation lead in your country.

One thing that is well worth figuring out in the early days of your startup is your "one-pager." As the name suggests, this is your business on a page, a quick reference guide that people can glance at and rapidly understand what you are doing. Having something clear and to the point allows you to include this document in emails, and you can quickly get back to people if they ask to see your "one-pager"!

Finally, with any of your networking efforts, you need to keep in mind that you are not looking for quick wins. Instead, your goal should be to build long-term relationships with people over the coming years. We keep a list of the 20 most important people in our network, and we make sure we are reaching out to them every month or at least once a quarter. We buy them presents for Christmas, Eid, Passover or send them books that have moved us. We send them nice emails asking about their families. We thank them publicly on social media. As much as you can, and without it becoming weird, treat them like royalty, because when the time comes where they want to buy your product, invest in you, buy your company, or tell their friends about you, it will all be worth it.

Selling your idea

From a practical point of view, how do you get out there and get people buying your idea?

Let's approach this from both the B2B and B2C perspectives. As a reminder, B2B is where you sell directly to businesses which then sell them on for you or use your product at scale (e.g., you sell your tomatoes to McDonalds, which then use them in their burgers). B2C is where you sell your product directly to individual customers (e.g., you have burger sauces that you want people to buy online through your website).

CHAPTER 12

With a B2B approach, you are trying your best to sell to the key decision-makers (e.g., the tomato buyers at McDonalds). Getting into a room with senior decision-makers at this level is largely going to be about networking. You are trying to get into the right "orbit" to figure out where the key leaders are playing and identify the sales of this nature that can add major boosts to your revenue. The easiest way to find these folks is to attend the big annual conferences or events for your sector, and exhibit if you can afford it. If you are lucky enough to get a meeting with someone who you are trying to sell to in a B2B sense, here is how we think you should try to make the most of that meeting:

- Get there early. If you are late, you've probably blown the meeting already. It doesn't matter if you live in Dhaka and it takes four hours to get there, or you live in Los Angeles and the traffic was bad that day. Get there on time. Or, if it is a video call, be there five minutes early and make sure your WIFI is strong and your device is fully charged!

- Think about what you are going to wear. If you are the funky, innovative company, dress the part. If you are the outdoor-focused company, feel free to wear your outdoor wear. If you are offering professional services like accounting or legal, wear a suit or at least look smart.

- Let them talk, and listen, for at least 60% of the time. Ask them what they are trying to achieve and tailor your offering accordingly during the meeting. Speak clearly about what you can provide, and either in the meeting or when you follow up, present your product offering and the price, with a couple of options (e.g., a lite and full package) that they could consider. Don't be afraid to up-sell them where you try to add in extra purchases that they hadn't been considering, as they may have more money to spend than you think.

- In the meeting, know when to push and when not to push. If you are feeling brave, you can be bold but polite in challenging their thinking (they may like that, or you may screw up the meeting!). Sometimes, though, if they are not connecting with your idea, acknowledge that right now you are not a good fit for them, thank them for their time, and offer to keep in touch. Be careful walking this line, and know that you are not just trying to get a short-term win but rather have them keep you in mind for years to come. If they like you in the meeting (even though they didn't buy from you immediately), there's a chance that a sale may pop up another time, but if they didn't like you, then you can be sure they will not likely reach out!

- Regardless of how the sales meeting went, try to follow up within 24 hours. You might have had an awesome connection, felt that they were excited, and are convinced that they want to buy a million dollars' worth of whatever you are selling. But it is not a sale until the money is in the bank, so close the deal as quickly as you can. Essentially, you want to get a proper proposal through to them (with a clear price and scope of works or list of goods), get it to contract (or a purchase order), and then to invoicing as quickly as possible. As the salesperson who is building the relationships, sometimes it can make sense to move this more transactional part of the deal to another member of your team (or at least a finance@ email address!) so that it can feel like just an administrative step for everyone, rather than being wrapped up in all the excitement and charisma that you brought to win the sale.

A B2C approach is slightly different.

Here you want to focus on your bullseye customer; essentially the kind of person who most often buys your product.

Sometimes this is your user, but not always.

An easy way to think about this is to consider who would be the bullseye customer for Google's search engine. Of course, there are billions of *users* of Google, but their bullseye customer is primarily the marketing professional who buys their ad services. At a shoe store, your bullseye customer is the person who likes to buy your shoes. At a children's health clinic, the user is the child getting support but the customer (the person who pays the bill) is their parent or guardian (or maybe even the health insurance company choosing which clinics they are aligned to). You want to learn as much as you can about your bullseye customer early on. Consider asking a bunch of questions, with the ones below as a start. This won't give you a perfect bullseye customer profile, and you may have to make some stereotypes here, but it's a useful exercise.

- Are your customers usually male or female? Or does gender not matter?
- How old are they?
- Are they everyday customers walking into a store, or are they employees in companies?
- Do they live in rural or urban areas?
- Are they educated?

- Are they rich or poor? How much do they make each month?
- Do they use mobile phones?
- Do they use social media? Which platforms?
- What do they like doing in their spare time?
- What excites them?
- What don't they like?
- What do they spend their money on?
- Do they access services in town?
- Do they read the newspaper? Listen to the radio? Which stations?
- Will they be excited by your work? Or do you have to inspire them?
- What is their name? (Come up with a name for your classic bullseye customer and think about them every time you try to sell your product or service!)

Of course, there are many more questions you could ask, but hopefully you get the idea! Once you've got a sense of your bullseye customer, figure out how you are going to find them, get your products in front of them, and thrill them. If you are finding them (i.e., they are coming to your website, store, or taking your meetings) but they are not buying, then figure out why and fix your product so it is more compelling for them!

Your ideal customers will very rarely just come to you. Instead, you need to market. Network. And, most importantly, have the courage to ask: "Would you like to buy this?"

Building your team

In the early days of your business, as we've mentioned a bunch of times, you will be doing almost everything yourself (and/or with your co-founder). But if the business starts to grow, you will have to build a team, and before long you may be spending a whole bunch of your time trying to manage and keep them! Here are some key questions to think about as this starts to take shape for you:

How big should your team be?

As small as possible to deliver on your product promises but still maximize your revenue and growth in a way that you can afford. We know plenty of people who love to boast about how big their teams have become, but we feel the most important thing to keep in mind is not the size of your team but their effectiveness. Don't be embarrassed if you have a team of three people, particularly if that team is making promising revenue and a big difference in the world. To link back to my (Aaron's) military days, I always say to not build an army but instead build a small special forces team – highly-skilled people with expertise in different areas but the ability to work well as a team. In the early days, bear in mind you don't have to necessarily bring people in as employees. For example, don't hire a full-time graphic designer, instead engage with an agency you love and hire them for the jobs you need. Hire a social media freelancer to do your social media posts three times a week. Hire a bookkeeper to look after your finances rather than jumping into trying to find an expensive CFO. Keep in mind that every person you hire will see you paying for their salary, their equipment and technology, and the power, toilet paper, and water they may use. Of course, if your revenue starts to slump, you also need to keep paying the salaries of your full-time and part-time staff, which can become very challenging very quickly. Also, if you are a profit social enterprise, the more money you spend on employees the less you will be able to direct to your social mission! By all means, hire amazing talent and grow your team later as the business grows; but in startup, keep things lean.

With all this in mind, who should you get to join your team?

We think that every team needs some visionaries who come up with ideas, analysts who critique those ideas, and implementers who make things happen. Chances are, as the founder, you will play the visionary role. Get some good analysts on board as mentors that you can run ideas by. But when you hire, we'd encourage you to hire doers, people who have an exceptional track record of getting things done, even if they are not perfectly trained in what you want them to be doing (you can teach them that). A great way to test for this is to actually give someone a task to do during the hiring process, such as, "What would your plan be to get our products into five more stores?" The best people won't just give you an analytical plan to do that, they'll call around to their friends and get you into a store. If you have a hunch someone might be good, consider bringing them in as a contractor for a week or a few months to see if they can do what you were hoping they might. In our teams, we often hire for cultural fit, asking ourselves whether this is someone who can bring positive energy to the team. To test for this during the interview phase, any new recruit gets to meet a good percentage of the team they might be working with (or, in a smaller company, the whole team). If existing staff don't have a good feeling about a potential hire, we pay close attention to that. We also hire slowly, meaning that if you work for one of our companies, you have usually made it through about five different types of interviews (with leadership, maybe spending a half day at the office to see how they fit in, joining a team brainstorming session, etc.). We are usually wary of people who only spend one or two years at each company, nervous that they will do the same with us. Finally, our favorite questions at interview are:

- When are you happiest professionally? What tasks are you doing when you find yourself in flow?

- What are you trying to improve about yourself? To get the best answer, we politely interrupt as they start their first response to ask for the second thing they are working on, then politely interrupt again and to ask for the third thing, which is usually where it gets interesting!

- What is the job you would leave this job for? This question gets to the heart of what really makes them tick, so don't let them just respond with, "This is my dream job!"

Once you've got a team, how do you keep them?

Anyone can hire a team, but it takes great leadership and management to keep one. We've always worked hard to keep our best people, and are proud that in many of our teams our best members have never left or have stayed for years. Some of our employees have gone on to become entrepreneurs and start their own businesses, which we love too! Here is what we have tried to focus on as bosses:

We make sure that everyone knows exactly what they should be doing with a clear job description that they understand. We also support them in that work, giving them extra mentoring, training, or assistance as they improve their effectiveness.

We set big goals as a team, clearly spell out the tasks we will all need to do to hit them, and then celebrate and reward people when they are reached. Rewards don't always have to be money – in the early days, a bottle of cheap sparkling wine and a plate of chocolate chip cookies always went a long way! Giving people the day off is a great reward as well, particularly when people have been working hard, or even getting really bold with four-day work weeks or nine-day fortnights.

We say thank you a lot. At least once a day to every team member. It's free to do, and people like to hear it!

We like to think that we have a lively culture and working in our teams is fun, and we have plenty of time for drinks and team hangouts. Saying that, we also respect everyone's time, so never contact anyone outside of work hours, and we put Friday drinks on at 4:00pm rather than eating into people's weekends by putting them on at 6:00pm. We say that family and health is more important than work, and encourage people to spend time with their families, pick up their children from school, and take lots of time off when they have babies.

We also trust our people and try not to micromanage them. We believe that outcomes are more important than time spent working, and encourage people to focus on the activities that will bring the results that we need.

Sometimes we know that we need to lead our teams, which is where we metaphorically climb up a tree to get some perspective and determine where the organization should be going. At other times, we need to manage, which is where we are metaphorically down in the jungle with everyone, sweating, bleeding, and fighting to move forward. We've found our teams respect someone who is willing to get their hands dirty and are inspired by someone with a powerful vision of where things are going, so we try to do both.

If you are a non-profit you may need to bring a board together, which is usually a group of volunteers who provide advice on the company and, ultimately, have decision-making power over the CEO. Or if you are a for-profit business, your investors may expect to join your board also. As a founder, when you are forming a board, think about finding a powerful chairperson who will do a good job of leading and managing the governance of the organisation. They don't need to be the most successful, the most impressive or the richest. They need to be good at governance. With the other board members, work to identify people who can give you potent (and free!) advice, information, and access to networks. Make an effort to find people with diverse backgrounds, genders, and perspectives. Research shows this leads to greater innovation, better decisions, and improved business outcomes. If you have some very high-profile people who can give you amazing advice, perhaps think about not bogging them down with a board seat. Instead, try to buy them lunch a few times a year so that you can run ideas by them. We've done this with a select few people, and their advice has literally changed our businesses and lives (hat tip to Andy Kuper of Leapfrog in particular). Many of our businesses do not have a board. Instead, we've decided to keep things lean, with decisions being made by the founders. This obviously changes as the companies get bigger though!

Regardless of whether your investors are on your board or not, treat them like your team and email at least monthly updates about what you have been up to, the big sales and finance numbers they will want to keep an eye on, and any asks that you have of them.

Lastly, (and noting that team culture is worthy of its own library of books, but this is merely a quick insight into some of what we have come to believe), we feel strongly that the only thing more powerful than ownership is authorship. This means that we let our team come up with much of the plan (we often do this at multi-day retreats, with plenty of good food, fun, and time to relax as a team), and give people big responsibility in their areas. In fact, if you work in our teams, you'll hear us say one line a lot: "You're the boss, what do you want to do?" The more your team feels like they created the strategy, the more they will make it happen.

Staying alive as a company

Finances and legal. These are the two things that can easily derail your business.

Let's start with finances.

Rule 1: Unless you are a brilliant accountant and bookkeeper yourself, you need to hire one, even if they are just a contractor.

Rule 2: Understand your burn rate, which is essentially how much money you are burning through each month to keep the company going. Keep this as low as you can early on, and do your best to not increase it with fixed costs that you can't get rid of easily and don't need (like leases on fancy offices, expensive employees, or unnecessary machinery).

Rule 3: Keep an eye on your runway, which is basically your money in the bank divided by your burn rate. For example, if your burn rate is US$20,000 a month, and you have US$100,000 in the bank, your runway is five months. If it gets below two months, you are looking very risky. If it is below a month, that's terrifying.

Rule 4: Write up a budget (which is what you think you will spend and make across a year) and explore what your worst-case and best-case scenarios look like. Then track the difference between your budget (what you think might happen) and your actuals (what is happening) to see whether you are closer to your best- or worst-case scenario. You may need to adjust your operations accordingly. If you don't know how to keep track of this, see Rule 1.

Rule 5: As early as possible, as a founder, separate your personal and business finances.

Rule 6: The money is not in the bank until the money is in the bank. Cash is incredibly hard to get, and very easy to spend, so work hard to close deals and have your invoices paid, and don't spend money on things you don't need (like fancy furniture for a cool new office in the trendiest suburb in town).

Rule 7: Diversify your revenue, so that you have at least five clients or more who make up your income. If you have only a small list of clients, one or two of them not renewing with you, or going with your competitor can be very damaging.

Rule 8: Be careful of big contracts. In fact, one of the most dangerous times for a company is when it moves from small to medium size. So, while that huge contract can be exciting to get, if you bring on huge expenses to meet it (like new machinery, extra staff, or a bigger space) and then that client bails on you, it could end your company. Aim to sign up to longer deals (even if you have to offer a discount), ask for 50% deposits before you start on the work, and have the courage to just say no if it is too risky.

Rule 9 (and the most important one):

DROOM.

Which stands for don't run out of money. As a business owner, have a good grasp of your finances (i.e., don't be the plane pilot who is in the back toilet reading a magazine). You should be looking months ahead, and take immediate and decisive action to address red flags.

Now, for the legal side. Make sure everything is above board. Avoid cutting corners with your legal structures because this gets harder to change later in the business. For example, if you are an events company, get the approvals you need to run the event legally. If you are a food company, get the approvals you need to make the food safely. When you hire people, sign them up to proper contracts that a lawyer has looked over. If you are offering anything with risk, have people sign the right liability forms. If you are issuing shares, do this in the appropriate manner from the beginning. Consider getting company director insurance cover. While you don't need to spend all your time mitigating risk, trust your gut and try to do the right thing. When all else fails, google the rules, ask a lawyer or the local government, and keep your conscience clean!

Looking after yourself

Finally, in the early days of your business, if you are burning out, then there is a real chance the business will too. So, you need to keep an eye on your wellbeing and ensure that you are staying happy and healthy. There has been a big push in recent years for entrepreneurs to keep wellbeing at the front of their mind. We fully embrace this change, but also know that if you want to move your business beyond a small, lifestyle company, there are times where you are going to be under stress and not a picture of perfect health and mindfulness. While we could list all the things you could be doing to operate at peak performance, we know that in the early days your wellbeing will suffer, so at the very least here are the things you should keep an eye on:

- Your own health. Try to keep track of the number days

you are grumpier than usual or tired for much of the day. If there's a downward turn, make some changes and commit to eating better, spending less time working, rebuilding your most important relationships, and keeping fit.

- Don't take pride in being a workaholic. Instead, take pride in getting loads of important work done and then resting. In all the years of starting and running businesses, we have rarely worked weekends or late into the night. There are no prizes for people who work the longest, but there are big rewards for those who work the smartest.

- Pay yourself. Too often, the founders of impact businesses don't look after their own lives. We've been guilty of this, and with several of our businesses have not paid ourselves or have been among the lowest paid people in the company. Don't follow our lead. As early as you can, start paying yourself – even if it is US$50 a week – then, as things improve steadily, increase your salary. It builds a good habit, keeps you motivated, and, in time, it will help you pay your rent too.

- Finally, don't forget the most important people in your life. If you build an impact business but lose your marriage, or your relationship, or all your friends, or connections with your family, that's not a great place to be. We have always said that our marriage is more important than any business we start, so where we've felt a tension, we've made changes quickly. We've ensured our friendship circles are separate from our businesses. And we've kept aside plenty of time for our family. In particular, since we've had kids, we've made sure that they get all the love and attention we can possibly give them. We were pretty inspired to hear Barack Obama once say that when he looked back on his life, the thing he would be most proud of would be his two daughters. We think that's awesome.

Keeping things fresh and growing

Lastly in this chapter, we want to encourage you to stay in this for the long haul.

Keep in mind that variety is the spice of life, and every year or so look at your job description and make sure you are doing the work you want to be doing (and remember, you don't always have to be the CEO, you can hire someone who is better at this than you!).

While you need to make sure that you keep delivering the classic products that your customers love to buy, don't be afraid to try to bring new products and services to market.

Try to have a team retreat with your leaders (or everyone in the team if you are small enough) at least once a year where you celebrate the wins, and address some big strategic issues, like:
 - ask "what should we start, stop, and keep doing?";
 - ask "what compelling offer will future competitors make to our customers?"; or
 - set some massive goals as a team and then innovate all the ways you can get there.

While your work might get old sometimes, and you might get tired, never forget why you started it all and the change you wanted to make. If you start to find it isn't fun anymore, make some changes.

1.	It is unacceptable that ✓
2.	We believe ✓
3.	But right now the reality is that ✓
4.	The root cause we are going to focus on is ✓
5.	The ideas ✓
6.	Test the best ✓
7.	Does it help to solve the problem in a scalable and sustainable way? ✓
8.	Pivot or persevere? ✓
9.	Turn your test into a real product ✓
10.	Turn your product into a company ✓
11.	Raising money ✓
12.	Running the business ✓

13

Chapter 13

This book is about starting a business that makes a difference.

Therefore, we think a fitting way to end is to help you keep on track with the impact you are making. Because, in the midst of all the busyness that comes with running a business, sometimes this can fall by the wayside.

Keeping track of your impact keeps you motivated. So the late nights, being told NO all the time, the stress of staff leaving, the anguish that comes when you have an unhappy customer, and every other issue you will face are much easier to suck up when balanced against the impact you are having.

Secondly, it is powerful for you to communicate this impact to your customers. If they know that you (and, by association, they) are making a difference with every purchase, you may inspire more loyalty from them, and they will feel like they are making a difference each time they buy from you.

Thirdly, it will motivate your team. If you can set a big, bold impact target, and make tangible steps towards it, it gives real purpose to each day for everyone.

Now, this can become very complex.

We both have multiple degrees in international and community development and advise branches of the United Nations, global companies, and foreign governments on impact, and even we can go a little cross-eyed when we try to get our head around the different approaches to impact assessment. So, as we have done throughout this book, we will keep things simple. Follow us step by step through the following basic approach to measuring the impact of your ventures.

Step 1: Use an impact database that already exists.

The most obvious one at the time of writing is the United Nation's Sustainable Development Goals (SDGs). These are basically 17 goals that have been set by all the UN member states, designed to make a significant dent into poverty levels around the world. Helpfully, they cover several categories including health and education, inequality, economic growth, and the environment. So, find the SDGs on the UN's website and figure out with which of them your impact is most aligned (we'd recommend no more than three to keep things simple).

Step 2: Determine your activities.

This is, quite simply, what you do. This might be running after-school learning programs for at-risk kids, or selling and installing solar panels or water purifiers, or providing health advice.

Step 3: Determine your outputs.

Outputs can be tricky to define as they are often confused with both "activities," which we just covered, and "outcomes," which we are about to cover. Essentially, outputs are the immediate results from your activities. This could include the number of panels installed if you were a solar energy company, or the number of community awareness/education events held if you were focused on health advocacy. These are the easiest things to measure as they are in your control and directly related to your activities.

Step 4: Determine your outcomes.

Where your outputs are short-term, immediate activities, your outcomes are the bigger, more long-term changes that you make. Essentially, what difference have you made to the world with your activities and outputs? For example, the outcomes of a company with the goal of increasing access to safe water and decreasing instances of waterborne diseases would be "the number of households that are now accessing safe drinking water" and "the reduction in the number of children suffering from diarrhea." For a solar panel company, an outcome might be "less indoor air pollution in homes" or "money saved on cooking fuel."

Outcomes change lives, so they are more important than outputs when assessing your overall impact. For example, if your activity is to spread the word about malaria, an output may be that your team puts up 10,000 educational posters across a city. The outcome of this work, however, may be an increase in mosquito net purchases in which leads to fewer malaria deaths each year.

You need to be excited about your data collection but also humble about what you are attributing to your work. For example, if you proudly put up your malaria posters, and then the next year there were fewer cases of malaria in the city, would it be fair to claim that your team made the difference? Maybe. But also, maybe not. Perhaps the weather conditions were better that year. Or another company brought a great new mosquito net to market. Or there was a new vaccine being trialed. Get excited about what you are doing, but don't be blinded by the feeling that it's all because of you.

Step 5: Determine your goals.

Once you have a sense of your activities, the outputs that come from these, and then the outcomes that you feel you can attribute fairly to your work, it is time to set some bold goals about the kind of change you are hoping to make. Think big here because ambitious goals can really excite people! For example, in the early days of one of our ventures that we co-founded, we said, "This work will help to change the lives of a million people living in poverty." It was a big goal, but it felt amazing when we hit it, and we had a few drinks to celebrate everyone's hard work.

Again, there is plenty more we could discuss on this topic, but we think this is enough to get you started. So, get yourself clear on the above, then start to get into the important work of doing those activities, to see those outputs, and, over time, beginning to proudly (yet humbly) document the outcomes and move towards your big goals.

1. It is unacceptable that ✓
2. We believe ✓
3. But right now the reality is that ✓
4. The root cause we are going to focus on is ✓
5. The ideas ✓
6. Test the best ✓
7. Does it help to solve the problem in a scalable and sustainable way? ✓
8. Pivot or persevere? ✓
9. Turn your test into a real product ✓
10. Turn your product into a company ✓
11. Raising money ✓
12. Running the business ✓
13. Make a difference ✓

14

Conclusion (but really it's just the beginning)

It's hard work starting and running a business that makes a difference.

But we think there is a process that you can follow, which we've outlined in this book, that can make it slightly easier for you.

One last time, let's walk through that process.

You started with identifying what it was that you were passionate about: your why. You then moved quickly into thinking about the future you were fighting for, and what success would look like if you could make a big difference in that area. You then moved back to the present, identifying the current reality to get a sense of what was happening. You broke this reality down into different root causes to try to get a better sense of the complexity of the issue. You spent some time determining which other players were already trying to solve this problem in order to not reinvent the wheel. After focusing on just one root cause, we helped you to innovate 50 potential solutions, the best of which you prototyped, and then took into the market to test. Following this test, you asked yourself some tough questions around whether your solution had the potential to help solve the root cause, and whether it was potentially scalable and sustainable, basically determining whether it was worth growing! Equipped with these insights, you were able to determine if you were going to pivot or persevere with the concept. If you were persevering, we then helped you to turn your test into a product, and then turn your product into a company. At the tail end of the book, we talked about how you could grow and raise capital, how you could run the business in a scalable and sustainable way and, ultimately, prove impact.

There is plenty to think about and do in the steps detailed above, and hopefully we've given you loads of practical advice to help you navigate your way through this journey you've decided to take.

We've found ourselves at the end of this journey a few times now, where we have led projects, non-profits, or companies and decided that it was time for us to move on. Some we've left, others we've closed, and, perhaps most excitingly, a few we've sold.

Bearing that in mind, here are some final words of encouragement, warning, and a dose of reality.

Firstly, and perhaps most importantly, don't forget your life in all of this. Your health, your happiness, your longevity, it matters, so protect it all. At the end of the day, you aren't much good to anyone and won't make an impact if you burn out. So, ensure that you are still smiling, still living, still taking time to laugh, cry, and enjoy life, because it will flash by in a moment.

Secondly, live a life where you give love and receive love. Decades from now, it's more likely that you will remember moments and experiences with your closest friends and family than you will a board meeting, a sale you made, or a new product you launched. So, keep plenty of time and space for those closest to you, because without them you don't have much.

And, finally, remember that you are leaving a legacy by starting this company. While you may rarely (if ever) hear it directly from people, lives are being changed because of what you started. Soon, if not already, someone will be living a healthier, happier, longer, or more fulfilling life because of what you do. We aren't old just yet, but will be one day, and we wonder if this quiet satisfaction that we made a difference may be one of the most fulfilling things about our life. We might think about Frank, who received an education through a school we ran. Or Mary, who started a pig farm that changed her family's income through a micro-loan we helped provide. Or the entrepreneur in Kenya in whom we invested (and talked some of our friends into doing the same). Or the mother who gave birth safely in a clinic we helped to build. Most of these people won't know our names, and we will never know all their individual stories. But we will know that out there, someone lived a little better because we tried to help.

Who will you help?

CONCLUSION (BUT REALLY IT'S JUST THE BEGINNING)

What will their stories be?

What will their names be?

Even if they are unable to thank you, we will now.

Thank you.

For caring.

For having the spark.

For doing what you do.

It matters. Very much.

"Few will have the greatness to bend history itself; but each of us can work to change a small portion of events, and in the total; of all those acts will be written the history of this generation."

– Bobby Kennedy

Also by Aaron Tait and Kaitlin Tait

Edupreneur - Unleashing Teacher-Led Innovation in Schools

If you can change education, you can change the world.

Edupreneur gives teachers the "how." You already know what needs to be done to improve education, but you may lack the support and processes to bring it to life—and that's where this book comes in. You'll walk through the four stages of innovation—dreaming, digging, making and sharing—and learn how to unleash ground-shaking change from the classroom up. Straightforward, highly practical and kick-in-the-pants inspirational, this book is your new companion for making education work. You'll read about passionate teachers who have raised attendance from 40% to 90%; you'll read about principals who took on the worst-performing schools and turned them around; you'll read about leaders who had the courage to take the reins of a school and turn it from good to great—and you'll learn how they did it and how you're entirely capable of the same kind of revolutionary change. This is a book not just for challenging schools, but for all educators who are passionate about providing a great education for every student, every day.

Dream Team - A Practical Playbook to Help Innovative Educators Change Schools

The world needs great individual educational changemakers capable of identifying problems and creating bold, scalable solutions. But the world also needs *Dream Teams* - groups of talented administrators, teachers, staff, students, and community members who are passionate about making things better for kids, believe that school-based change is the means to this end, and are willing to roll up their sleeves and work together to achieve it.

This book is for Dream Teams in the making. In it, global education leaders Aaron Tait and Dave Faulkner share the models and methods of 10 brilliant leadership teams at urban, suburban, and rural schools in the United States, Canada, Australia, and New Zealand. Informed by these successes, the authors provide specific, sometimes audacious advice for navigating what they call the Change Leader Journey: how to move from Dream Team assembly and problem analysis all the way through to solution generation, piloting, promotion, and evaluation. Innovative educators come in all forms, and they require lots of options. Here, you'll find a collection of practical ideas and tools designed to fuel transformational leadership without sacrificing instructional excellence or anyone's sanity. Whether your team is a group of fearless rebels, more cautious types, or somewhere in between, Tait and Faulkner's flexible approach can help you figure out where you want your school to go, build a more collaborative and creative culture, and generate the solutions that best serve your students.

Printed in the USA
CPSIA information can be obtained
at www.ICGtesting.com
LVHW020440111224
798785LV00004B/499